IDOL
LIES

How Jesus is setting us free from...

IDOL
LIES

Facing the Truth
About Our
Deepest Desires

Dee Brestin

AUTHOR OF THE MILLION-COPY BESTSELLER *THE FRIENDSHIPS OF WOMEN*

WORTHY®
PUBLISHING

Copyright © 2012 by Dee Brestin

Published by Worthy Publishing, a division of Worthy Media, Inc., 134 Franklin Road, Suite 200, Brentwood, Tennessee 37027.

WORTHY is a registered trademark of Worthy Media, Inc.

HELPING PEOPLE EXPERIENCE THE HEART OF GOD

eBook available at www.worthypublishing.com

Audio distributed through Oasis Audio; visit www.oasisaudio.com

Library of Congress Control Number: 2012941809

Unless otherwise indicated, Scripture quotations are from *The Holy Bible, English Standard Version.* Copyright © 2001 by Crossway Bibles, a division of Good News Publishers.

Scripture quotations marked CEV are from the Contemporary English Version®. Copyright © 1995 American Bible Society. All rights reserved.

Scripture quotations marked KJV are from the King James Version. Public domain.

Scripture quotations marked MSG are from *The Message.* Copyright © 1993, 1994, 1995, 1996, 2000, 2001, 2002. Used by permission of NavPress Publishing Group.

Scripture quotations marked NEB are from the New English Bible. Copyright © Oxford University Press and Cambridge University Press, 1961, 1970.

Scripture quotations marked NIV are from the Holy Bible, *New International Version®,* NIV®. Copyright © 1973, 1978, 1984, 2011 by Biblica, Inc.™ Used by permission of Zondervan. All rights reserved worldwide.

Scripture quotations marked NKJV are from the New King James Version. Copyright © 1982 by Thomas Nelson, Inc. Used by permission. All rights reserved.

Scripture quotations marked NLT are from the *Holy Bible, New Living Translation,* copyright © 1996, 2004. Used by permission of Tyndale House Publishers, Inc., Carol Stream, IL 60188. All rights reserved.

Published in association with Creative Trust Literary, 5141 Virginia Way, Suite 320, Brentwood, TN 37027; www.creativetrust.com

For foreign and subsidiary rights, contact rights@worthypublishing.com

ISBN: 978-1-61795-072-8 (hardcover w/ jacket)
ISBN: 978-1-61795-367-5 (trade paper)

Cover Design: Faceout Studio, Jeff Miller
Cover Image: Shutterstock
Interior Typesetting: Susan Browne

Printed in the United States of America

12 13 14 15 16 17 SBI 8 7 6 5 4 3 2 1

To my sisters who piloted this study and

opened their hearts to the Stonecutter's knife.

_____

I will give you a new heart

and put a new spirit in you;

I will remove from you your heart of stone

and give you a heart of flesh.

———————

Ezekiel 36:26, NIV

CONTENTS

PART I

The Stonecutter

The heart is deceitful above all things,

and desperately sick;

who can understand it?

———————

Jeremiah 17:9

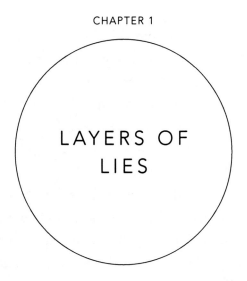

CHAPTER 1

LAYERS OF LIES

I've got layers of lies I don't even know about.

—Sara Groves, "Eyes Wide Open"

My name is Dee and I am an idolater.

For most of my Christian life I didn't *know* I was an idolater. I certainly didn't worship statues. I loved the One True God. But I have come face to face with my naïveté. I now know I have what Ezekiel calls "idols of the heart."

Let me tell you my story.

STONES IN OUR HEARTS

All I knew was that I was having trouble keeping an administrative assistant. I couldn't understand it.

Wasn't I a warm and caring boss? I never yelled or made unreasonable demands. Why didn't they appreciate what they had? The work was meaningful, the travel exciting, the pay good, and the boss encouraging. So what was the matter?

Since it took a good year to learn the complexities of the position, I would hire only someone who expressed a desire to work in the ministry long term. Yet invariably, after just two or three years, my assistant would have a change of heart about being involved long term and resign.

When my fourth administrative assistant resigned, I lamented to my friend Jan Silvious, expecting a sympathetic ear. Instead, she arched an eyebrow, peered at me through her funky rhinestone glasses, and said, "Dee, this seems to be a pattern in your life."

What? Was she implying that I was the problem?

That was a wake-up call for me. I had deceived myself about the darkness lurking in my heart. I told myself I was a good boss. But I wasn't.

All along, I had felt I was serving God. I was puzzled. *Why am I not experiencing more of the promised joy? Why do my assistants keep leaving?* In other words, before I became aware of my idolatry, I became aware of the symptoms telling me that something was not right.

As I would discover, I had idols in my heart that were blocking my intimacy with God, bringing friction in key relationships, and destroying my joy. Yet because soul idols are invisible, I didn't even know they were there.

Any time our deepest desire is for something other than God because we think *that* will satisfy or rescue us, a dangerous "soul idol" is forming. We may idolize the approval of people, our own comfort, or maintaining control. All of these things can become "idol lies," things we value more than God. We cling to these idols, and in so doing, as Jonah said, we "forfeit the grace that could be ours" (see Jonah 2:8, NIV).

The scriptural truth on which this book is based has had an enormous impact on my own life and gives me a passion for you to know it too. I have tested the truth in pilot groups, and the results in women's lives are nothing less than astounding. Though many of these women are mature believers, a light is going on that has been off all of their Christian lives. They are being delivered from anxiety, depression, gluttony, and so many destructive behaviors and emotions.

Let me share with you an image that has been helpful to these women and to me on this journey: soul idolatry is like cancer, especially the silent cancers. My husband did not know he had a tumor in his colon, but he did know that his stomach was often upset and that he felt unusually tired. He told me that he might have an ulcer and that he would check that out, but he believed that he really just needed a good vacation. He did not know a malignant tumor was in his body, growing, destroying—that it would take him from our five children and me in his prime.

Tumors are hard lumps like stones. What is so frightening about them is that, left unchecked, they *grow*. The sooner we discover them, the better our chance of rescue.

And God is on the move, uncovering these hidden stones in our hearts and chiseling them down. I call Jesus the Stonecutter because He can reveal, remove, and replace our heart idols with Himself.

Jan's comment about "the pattern in my life" helped me see my "stone," my calcifying tumor. I wanted this malignancy out so badly that I submitted to the work of the Stonecutter. And though the surgery was hard, my color is coming back, and I see a radical difference in my relationships. I am experiencing the healing that comes after a successful surgery, when a foreign body is removed and living flesh can thrive again.

Jesus the Stonecutter can transform your life as well.

Every believer needs to be set free, and it begins with getting past our denial, with seeing what we really idolize, and admitting this to God and to others. We may think, for example, that our deepest desire is for God, but in reality we are running to food, friendship, or Facebook to fill up our souls. We may think that our identity is in Christ, but in reality it may be in the success of our ministry, mothering, or marriage.

Just as the only hope an alcoholic has of being set free is seeing and confessing his real problem, so it is with us.

And so I stand before you and confess.

MY NAME IS DEE AND I AM AN IDOLATER

Each time an administrative assistant resigned, my diagnosis was that there was a problem with my assistant.

I needed help to see myself as I really was. Jeremiah tells us our hearts are deceitful and desperately wicked (Jeremiah 17:9). Solomon tells us that our hearts are like deep, dark waters—but a friend of understanding can draw those waters out (Proverbs 20:5). When my friend Jan challenged my assessment of my situation, her words helped me see the idols lurking in the dark waters of my soul.

All of us need help to see ourselves as we really are. We can look in a mirror several times a day and not be shocked, and then someone hands us a photograph. *Whoa! I have to change my hair . . . lose weight . . . never wear that dress again . . .*

This is why God tells us we so desperately need the body of Christ. (It is also why there is an accompanying Bible study for small groups at the back of this book.) God gave us to each other to help us see what we cannot see on our own and to encourage one another as we travel together in the same journey—the journey of being set free.

So my conversation with Jan was the beginning of my recognizing that something might be wrong with *me*, not the people who worked for me. Yet I needed more evidence. God gave that to me through a story. A story can open our eyes because it has the power to bypass our natural defenses and slip right into the heart.

That's what happened when Nathan came to King David, who, amazingly, was in denial about his sins of sexual abuse and murder.[1] Nathan told him a story about someone else, a rich man who took a poor man's only lamb, a lamb he loved "like a daughter," and killed it, serving it for dinner. David was incensed and said, "As the LORD lives, the man who has done this deserves to die" (2 Samuel 12:5).

Nathan said to David, "You are the man!" (verse 7).

Finally David saw. We see his response of genuine repentance in Psalm 51.

After Jan's comment jolted me awake, God sent me my own Nathan through a sermon by Jim Om titled "Models of Manipulation."[2] He spoke about the story of Mary sitting at the feet of Jesus, "hanging on every word he said" (Luke 10:39, MSG), and of Martha boiling with anger as she works alone in the kitchen, finally bursting out with confrontation for Jesus and her sister.

You may have heard this story so often that your eyes glaze over when you hear it coming. I find Christian women think they already know the point of the passage. But do we? I've spoken and written about this story, but this time I heard it differently. *So please read the following carefully, even if you think you already understand this story.*

This is a story about idolatry and how it keeps us from Jesus.

MARTHA THE MANIPULATOR

How often I've heard women say, "I'd like to be a Mary, but I'm such a Martha." They think this is a story about trying hard to have the temperament of a Mary when God gave them the temperament of a Martha. It's not. Or they think it is a story about how sitting at Jesus' feet is more important than serving. But it is not about that either, because *both* are vital in the vibrant and balanced Christian life.

As Pastor Om pointed out, Martha had a heart idol, and the symptom of it was manipulation. He said one of the following signs occurs when a manipulator is in action:

1. An attempt to produce guilt
2. An unreasonable demand

When Martha comes charging out of that kitchen, her body language alone could have heaped a load of guilt upon her sister. But then she speaks "over" her sister and accuses the Lord: "Lord, do you not care that my sister has left me to serve alone?" (Luke 10:40). Then she makes her demand, barking an order to the Son of God: "Tell her then to help me."

So we see the symptoms of an idol in Martha—irritability, anxiousness, manipulation, and friction in her relationships. What is her heart idol, the deep desire that ruled her words and actions more than love for Jesus? Pastor Om thinks it may have been human *approval*. If Martha truly is the Martha Stewart of biblical days, this visit from an important guest is her chance to shine. Perhaps she is stomping the grapes for the wine, slicing the cucumbers for the salad, and steaming the red snapper over the fire—so yes, she is stressed! She is also miffed at Mary, who seems oblivious to all that has to be done.

There was a time when I was quite sympathetic with Martha, thinking it unfair that she had to fix a meal for thirteen men by herself while Mary sat at the feet of Jesus. But if you look carefully at the pronouns in the text, it is possible that Jesus came alone. That's how Walter Wangerin imagines it in his novel *The Book of God*: "During these last three years He has usually come in the company of His disciples. He first makes sure they all have food and places to sleep in Bethany. Then He silently slips into our courtyard."[3]

So if Jesus is alone, why is Martha in such a state preparing the meal? Charles Swindoll puts it like this: "Martha, Martha—chips and dip would be fine!"[4]

Or it may have been that Martha's heart idol, her deepest desire, is to remain in *control*. She is a natural leader—and leaders often think they know better than anyone else how things should be done. Even when praying, they are telling the Lord who made the galaxies just how things should be done.

I know how easy this is to do.

DEE THE MANIPULATOR

When I listened to this sermon, I was cut to the heart, for I saw myself. When I would be unhappy with something an assistant did or didn't do, I let my irritability rise instead of taking it before the Lord and asking Him for insight. Was this really a problem worth mentioning? Was there something else going on in my relationship with God that was producing my irritability?

Instead, like Martha, I let the simmering in me come to a boil. I was not as likely to lash out, but I would often mention a concern "sideways." If my assistant arrived late for work, for instance, I might ask if everything was okay at home. This made me look sympathetic, but in reality I was making a jab about her lateness, asking her sideways to explain her tardiness. If she didn't, and innocently responded, "Yeah. Everything's good," I would be irked! *She missed my meaning.* Then my icy body language communicated disapproval.

It wasn't effective and it made her feel beaten down. So why did I do it? I did it because my heart is desperately wicked and I couldn't see the stone in my soul. I justified my behavior.

When Jim Om told this story, it was as if he handed me a photograph. It was hard to face my ugliness, to admit I had a tumor growing—but I am so thankful to God for showing me my cancer. He is radiating this tumor, but I also know I must keep coming to Him, for my tumor has a frightening capacity to regenerate.

One of the idols that calls most loudly to me is *control*. I often feel I know what is best. Like Martha, I was a micro-manager, thinking I knew how things should be run. I wanted a detailed accounting of how my assistant spent her time. Gaye was my first full-time assistant, and she was particularly gifted and devoted to the ministry. Yet I still felt the need to be in control. If I observed something that seemed amiss (as Martha observed Mary's absence in the kitchen), I often failed to slow down and look at my own heart and be still before the Lord. Instead, I jumped to my own defense, going over in my mind why Gaye was wrong and why I was right.

I remember a period when Gaye's closest friend was facing a crisis that involved continual and life-threatening surgeries for her young son. They lived three hours away and Gaye wanted to be at her side each time for surgery and recovery. I should have listened to Gaye more carefully and, even more so, to the Lord. Instead, I was "worried and anxious" about many things: *Gaye doesn't really care about the ministry. There is so much work to be done—how can we get it done with her taking off like this all the time? I'm feeling overwhelmed. She needs to be here more, or things are going to fall apart.*

The truth is, Gaye cared deeply about the ministry, but she also cared about her friend. She *had* done what was absolutely needed for the upcoming retreat, and she was asking for grace in this time of need.

The stone god in my heart, this boulder *control*, was producing irritability, anxiousness, and manipulation. I wasn't really seeing Gaye as Jesus saw her, as a caring person deeply hurting for her closest friend. I didn't feel I could tell Gaye not to go on a mission of mercy, but I did manage to make her feel guilty with a passive-aggressive remark or a sigh. Gaye began to feel frustrated and unappreciated.

God had provided me with a wonderful woman, and if I had given her grace and freedom, she might have stayed on with the ministry, or at the very least I would have known that I wasn't the reason she left. I also missed the chance to see God work. If I had been still before Him, listening to Him and allowing *Him* to be my control, who knows what good fruit would have been produced?

MARTHA, MARTHA

Whenever a name is uttered twice in the Bible, it indicates passion. David mourned over his son's body, crying: "O my son Absalom, O Absalom, my son, my son!" Jesus looked over Jerusalem and cried, "O Jerusalem, Jerusalem . . . How often would I have gathered your children together as a hen gathers her brood under her wings, and you were not willing!" And Jesus pleads with Martha: "Martha, Martha, you are anxious and troubled about many things, but one thing is necessary" (Luke 10:41–42).

What would cause Jesus to use the double invocative with Martha? He sees her stone. He knows how it hurts her, how it weighs her down, how it robs her of peace and joy. His tone, I'm convinced, is compassionate rather than condemning.

God knows that the stones in our hearts are painful. They destroy relationships and ministries and keep us from experiencing Him. When He sees the stones in our hearts, He is grieved. He wants to remove them so that life can flow.

So Jesus reminds Martha that Mary has chosen the most important thing, which is to love the Lord with all our heart and with all our soul and with all our might (Deuteronomy 6:5).

The irony is that both Martha and I would have said we were serving God. And yet we were both working at cross-purposes with Him because we were not allowing Him to be in control. And we suffered. We were anxious, irritable, and missing the sweetness of Him. We also hurt other people.

Jesus wants us to turn from our paltry gods and trust Him to be our *comfort*, our *control*, and our *approval*. As the Stonecutter, He will break the painful stones of our heart and replace them with Himself. Ezekiel promises that God will change our heart of stone to a heart of flesh. When the stone "god" is removed, God's Spirit is no longer grieved, and He comes to reign in us, producing glorious fruit.

When we see Martha, later, at a party in celebration of the raising of her brother, Lazarus, she still has the type-A temperament and the gift of serving that God gave her. None of that has changed, nor should it. What has changed is that a stone has been removed from her heart so that her temperament and her gift are now being used as God intended. They are glorifying Him instead of feeding the stone tumor that was destroying her intimacy with God.

DEE, DEE

My sin of manipulation is fading and I am quicker to recognize when my idol of control is operating. Manipulative thoughts still come to mind, but I recognize them now as the enemies they are, and I am quicker to turn from them, to talk to my soul about God's love and wisdom, and then relinquish control to Him.

I know I am changing, and people are telling me so. My eldest daughter keeps saying, "Mom, you are *so* much better!" I feel a bit like the woman who has lost some weight and is told, "Wow, you look *so* much better—you have lost a *ton* of weight!" But, in truth, I *have* lost a ton of weight. My stone was Mount Everest.

My son-in-law is now my administrative assistant. When I first considered hiring him, he, my youngest daughter (his wife), and I prayed long and hard about it, for my record was not good. Would I bear fruit worthy of repentance?

We went along swimmingly for the first year and a half. I was ecstatic. (I do have a fine son-in-law who is full of talent, grace, and godliness.) Then, the second summer, we hit our first rough patch. He and my daughter were visiting me at our cabin in Wisconsin. David was continuing to work half days on his vacation, both on my ministry and with his own website company. Summer is a slow time for retreats, so he really didn't have a lot to do for me. Yet it seemed he was spending nearly all his time on his other business. My stone began to regenerate, and I began to regress to my old habit of going over in my mind why I was right and why he was wrong. I suggested we set a time to meet the next day and talk about a concern

I had. I noticed he seemed surprised, a red flag to me that my idol might be operating. The fact that I was tense was another red flag. I've learned that we should pay attention to our body language, for an increased heart rate, a tightening in our neck, or a clenching of our hands all may signal that our idol may be taking over.

I slowed down. I asked God to take over. I asked Him to help me to listen to Him. I prayed, as David did after Nathan had shown him a story picture of his idol: "Create in me a clean heart, O God, and renew a right spirit within me" (Psalm 51:10). I needed discernment—was I setting reasonable boundaries as a boss should, or was my stone returning? (They grow back, you see, for our hearts, as Calvin said, "are idol-making factories.")

Just before my scheduled meeting with David, I felt a strong prompting to turn to a devotional I'd been reading by Paul Tripp on Psalm 51 called *Whiter Than Snow*. So though David knocked on my door for our appointment, I asked him to give me another ten minutes.

I then turned to the reading for the day and this is what I read:

I am too skilled
at mounting
plausible arguments
structured
to make me feel okay
about what I think
what I desire

what I say
what I do.
I am too defensive. . . .

In the holy of holies,
Where I stand naked,
All covering gone,
Before You . . .
May you do there,
What I cannot do. . . .
May you create in me,
A clean heart.[5]

That was my *Dee, Dee*. When David returned, I was in tears. I'd been humbled. I'd seen my stone and experienced the Stonecutter's painful chisel. I told David how I had prayed and then what had happened. I confessed to him, "I am so quick to judge, so quick to justify myself and to blame others. I have done that this week with you, and I'm sorry."

At that moment, the Spirit of the Lord moved in—so real, so tangible. I saw David's facial expression change, soften. Humbly and graciously, he said, "Oh, Dee, I'm the same way."

The whole atmosphere changed. The Holy Spirit was no longer grieved and instead offered peace and wisdom. David and I were confessing our sins to one another and asking God to change us. We began talking with one heart and one mind about how to better serve the Lord in this ministry that belonged to Him. We relinquished control to Him and it made all the difference.

David is still working part-time with me, and I am so thankful for him. If and when we part, I am determined it will be because God is leading us in that way, not because my idols are driving him out.

FREE INDEED

One of the rich promises Jesus spoke was this: "If the Son sets you free, you will be free indeed" (John 8:36). So should we not wonder why some believers in Jesus Christ are set free from besetting sins and others remain chained? Each group seems to know the Lord, each group wants to change, but only one does. Though the chained group is weary of repeating their failures and weary of wilderness wanderings, they are stuck. In despair, they cry:

I don't want to be so anxious, but I can't seem to change.

I've been in counseling for years about forgiving my father, but I'm stuck.

I've tried so many times to lose weight and keep it off—it's hopeless!

Discouragement can lead to settling for a mediocre Christian life with occasional picnics in the desert. But that is not God's heart for us!

Indeed, a fresh wind is blowing through the body of Christ, from Africa to America, from Presbyterians to Pentecostals. A generation ago, most Christians were blind to their idolatry— we assumed idols meant golden calves and stone statues, and we didn't have any of those around our houses! *Christianity Today* reported that when George Barna asked individuals if they had broken the first commandment (to have no other gods before God), 76 percent said they had not.[6] But I know that statistic is drastically reduced today because believers are learning about heart idols. Tim Keller of Redeemer Presbyterian in New York City was a catalyst for reviving these truths, and now you find this teaching expounded in an increasing number of seminaries, pulpits, and books.

This mighty wind is awakening God's slumbering children to see what has kept them from transformation. The first step is seeing the treacherous stones lurking beneath the deep waters of our souls—stones that have stymied our journey and cut us to pieces. God's light is shining down into the deep, dark waters, revealing the Scylla that has shipwrecked lives.[7] In response, many are crying out to the Stonecutter, asking Him to remove the stones. And He's doing it. Grudges are being abandoned, weight is being lost, despair is dissipating, and an amazing excitement is rippling out, the joy so characteristic of revival. This is working! Why?

ATTACKING THE ROOT PROBLEM

So often we have failed to conquer a besetting sin because we have attacked the symptoms of our sin instead of its cause. Alcoholics Anonymous knows that there is no hope for deliverance until an alcoholic sees and names her *root* problem. As long as she denies her alcoholism and instead tries to overcome the symptoms it creates, such as a bad temper, frequent accidents, or absenteeism at work, she will not have victory. She must come to the point where she can stand up before a group and admit, "My name is Jane and I am an alcoholic." Managing symptoms does not work. The beast inside must be slain.

In the same way, unless we as believers identify the root problem that leads to a multitude of surface sins, we are doomed to failure. Though our surface sins are many, they spring from a small number of deep heart idols. As we touched on earlier, there are three basic categories of deep idols that, though not comprehensive, cover most of our heart problems. They are:

- Control/power
- Affirmation/approval
- Comfort/security[8]

Why does understanding our root problem free us when other plans fail? Consider: Someone with the deep idol of comfort/security may want to overcome overeating, overspending, or oversleeping. She sets new resolutions, for she wants to lose weight, to be free of debt, or to get out of bed and start her day with the Lord. The usual approach is to attack the surface sin: "I'll get a better diet, a better budget, or a better alarm clock." But her *deep* idol of comfort will cry out when it is restricted. It will tell her lies: *Just one potato chip . . . just window-shop . . . just a little more sleep . . .* It is crouching at the door, waiting for her to open it a crack, and when she does, it barrels in, slipping its chains around her.

It is not enough to attack the near sin. The "god" producing that sin must be destroyed. But it is important for you to know that this is not an easy fix. The false god has many disguises, often appearing as something positive in your life. It takes time to see him and name him. And yet, when you finally do, you will be halfway to victory.

You will also begin to see how idolatry motivates *everyone*, and find it appearing *everywhere* in Scripture. The metaphors God uses to illumine idolatry are rich and varied. Idolaters are compared to slaves (John 8:34) or addicts (Jeremiah 2:25) because they are in bondage; to blind people (John 9:39–40) because they are deceived; and to adulteresses (Hosea 2:13) because they are being unfaithful to God. Our heart idols are compared to stones (Ezekiel 36:26) because they weigh us down and block His Spirit, yet those stones are not inanimate, but alive, malignant, and hungry—like crouching beasts waiting to devour us (Genesis 4:7).

If my husband had seen his cancerous tumor a year before he did, I believe he could have won the battle. As long as we don't know we have a malignancy, we aren't even fighting. We are like the sleeping soldier who is easy prey to the approaching enemy.

I want to help you see the stone "gods" in your heart. I know that doesn't sound like fun. It sounds like going to the dentist. But I promise you, getting the rottenness out will bring health to your soul and dramatically change your life. The stone you thought was your friend is not your friend. He only pretends to be.

I think I can help you to understand this through Christy's story. Christy is one of my former assistants, and she has forgiven me for my manipulative ways. Our relationship is truly healed. Though we live an hour's drive apart, we will often meet in the middle at a quiet restaurant to break bread together and share the depths of our hearts: laughing, loving, and helping one another find strength in God.

Christy understands idols of the heart because she came to see her own, lurking in the deep waters of her soul. Her idol brought incredible pain into her life, but it took time for her to see it because it crouched, disguising itself as a friend.

But it was not. It was a cancerous stone. It has been destroyed and Christy has been set free.

Let me tell you Christy's story.

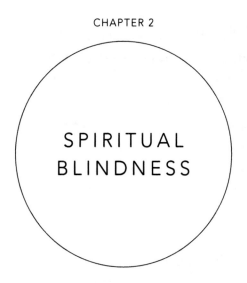

CHAPTER 2

SPIRITUAL
BLINDNESS

*Above everything else, avoid making a premature
claim that your blindness has been healed.*

—Dr. Martyn Lloyd-Jones, *Spiritual Depression*

Sometimes Christy will fill in for David at a retreat or come when I speak locally. We've both noticed how often when we arrive the coordinators will say, "We're praying women will get saved." We know they are praying that women will be saved from the *penalty* of sin, and we are too, but we also pray for believers to be saved from the *power* of sin. Being released from the *penalty* (the guilt) of sin is instantaneous, happening the moment we respond to God's call and to the payment Christ made for us at the cross. As Christy and I know in our own lives, being released from the *power* of sin is gradual, for bondage has layers. Being satisfied with being delivered from the penalty of sin is to settle for the lesser life, for the occasional picnic in the desert. Seeking release from the *power* of sin means recognizing the idol lies that keep us from God and allowing the Stonecutter to replace them with Himself.

Medical doctor and pastor Dr. Martyn Lloyd-Jones believed that the primary cause of so many Christians being perpetually in the doldrums was due to the fact that they did not understand the *double* power of the gospel to save.[9] The hymn "Rock of Ages" puts it like this:

> Be of sin the double cure
> Cleanse me from its guilt and pow'r.[10]

The story of the blind man brought to Jesus in Mark's Gospel is a wonderful illustration of our need for a "double cure." When Jesus laid hands on the man and asked him if he could see, the man replied, "I see people, but they look like trees, walking" (Mark 8:24).

Then Jesus laid His hands on his eyes again, and this time, when the blind man opened his eyes, he saw everything clearly. Of course this doesn't mean that Jesus failed the first time, but that His miracle is also a parable. The man experienced healing instantly, but his complete delivery from blindness was gradual.

All of us have hidden idols that need to be revealed, removed, and replaced. Christians who talk as if they have arrived may be the most blind of all.

So it was for Christy.

CHRISTY'S HIDDEN IDOLS

I told a little of Christy's story in *The Friendships of Women*, and if she travels with me to a retreat, I'll often bring her up and interview her because I know how women resonate with the problem she had. God made women to be particularly gifted in relationships, planning for us to bring warmth and healing in a cold and hurting world. But we easily turn gifts into gods. Friendship, food, sex—all can be distorted when we desire them too much.

Christy wasn't involved with drugs or illicit sex at college—she would have known that was wrong. She was immersed in friendship with sisters in Christ. What could be wrong with that? After all, at first our idols *seem* to bring us the comfort, approval, and security we crave.

Christy remembers the joy she had in the beginning of her college years, before her idols turned on her and began to cut her to pieces. She says,

> Though I was a Christian, when I started attending a Christian group on campus, I met women who integrated their faith in every area of their lives, who knew Jesus not just as their Savior, but also as their Lord. How bold they were in their faith! I was pleased when two of them, Lori and Sarah, asked me to room with them the next year. Sarah and I were both on sports' scholarships and became particularly close. How blessed I felt to have someone who knew me on a spiritual level—someone I connected with more deeply than I ever had before. It

meant so much when Sarah affirmed me, and when I sensed she needed me as I did her.

Christy's friendship with Sarah brought many gifts, but it also fed—rather than satisfied—Christy's deep desires for affirmation and security. She wanted someone to need her, to love her, and to be there for her. The more Sarah validated Christy through friendship, the more dependent Christy became on that friendship. But as the old hymn "The Solid Rock," says:

> I dare not trust the sweetest frame,
> But wholly lean on Jesus' name.
> On Christ the solid Rock I stand,
> All other ground is sinking sand.[11]

As dear and as godly as friends are, they cannot promise to always be there for us. They may let us down, because they, like us, are sinners. They may move away, fail us in our hour of need, or even die.

In fact, Sarah graduated that May. She would not be returning to college. Not only that, but she was engaged to be married. It would be a double parting. Christy recalls, "I remember vividly how sad I was. I didn't think I'd ever stop crying. I drove myself home for the summer break and cried all the way. My heart felt totally broken. I felt such a loss and I didn't think I could ever be as happy at college without Sarah being there."

One of the clearest ways to identify our idols, our deepest desires, is to ask, "What, if you lost it, would make you feel like life was unbearable?" Counselor David Powlison says a good way to identify our idols is to turn the commands to love God, to seek God, to fear God, and to trust God upside-down, asking ourselves, "What do we *really* love, what do we *really* seek, what do we *really* fear, and what do we *really* trust?"[12]

But Christy could not yet see, partly because what she loved seemed to be a good thing.

TURNING GIFTS INTO GODS

A Greek word turns up repeatedly in the New Testament whenever the subject of heart transformation comes up. It is *epithumia*, which could be translated as "too big" or "inordinate" (*epi*) and "desire" (*thumia*).

Our desires are not necessarily for destructive things such as cocaine or an adulterous affair, but we often have inordinate desires for God's good gifts, thus turning those gifts into little gods. We think about them, long for them, run to them, and face panic if we cannot get them or hold on to them.

Note the concept of *too much* in these proverbs, as the author repeatedly warns that a good thing can become destructive when our desire for it is too great.

If you find honey, eat just enough—
too much of it, and you will vomit.
(Proverbs 25:16, NIV)

Seldom set foot in your neighbor's house—
too much of you, and they will hate you.
(Proverbs 25:17, NIV)

Do not join those who drink too much wine
or gorge themselves on meat.

(Proverbs 23:20, NIV)

Don't let me be . . . too rich.
Give me just what I need.
If I have too much to eat,
I might forget about you.

(Proverbs 30:8–9, CEV)

Do you see the pattern? When a person takes a good gift from God like sweets, friendship, wine, meat, or money and allows it to become too important to her, it can lead to destruction. God intends for us to enjoy gifts when He gives them, keep them in moderation, and let them lead us to thank Him and worship Him. But because our hearts are "idol-making factories," we find ourselves worshiping the gift and forgetting God. We are idolaters at heart.

Christy had made her friends the most important thing to her, and this pattern continued in her life because she didn't see the danger. It was over ten years later when she let God help her to see.

IDOLS EXPOSED

By this time, Christy was a professional career woman with a great deal of responsibility who traveled across the country with her work. She was involved in a good church and had a circle of friends. One of those friends was Brooke, who quickly became a "kindred spirit" friend. When Christy shares at my retreats, the listening women nod in understanding as she tells them:

> You know the excitement you feel when you meet another woman with whom you really click? You feel like you've known each other forever, you're finishing one another's sentences, and you so look forward to time together because it so refreshes you. That's how I felt when I met Brooke. We often spoke by phone and emailed almost daily. When Brooke's day as a teacher ended, if I didn't hear, "You've got mail" on my computer, I would begin to question what Brooke's thoughts were, or what she might be doing with the rest of her day.

That year Christy planned a New Year's Eve party. Brooke had begun dating a man at church whom Christy had admired at one time, and Christy began to dread how she'd feel when Brooke brought him to the party. That night, not only did Christy feel the pain of romantic jealousy, but also the jealousy that this man was getting to spend a significant amount of time with Brooke—time that Brooke would no longer have for Christy. The next day Christy felt ill. She stayed on the sofa for three days, thinking she had the flu.

A few days later, another of Christy's friends approached her and said, "Christy, you don't have the flu. You have a problem with expecting too much from your friendship—and it's become a pattern in your life. You need help." The friend gave Christy the name and number of a Christian counselor who had helped her. She told Christy she would call the next day to make sure she made an appointment.

Christy remembers the pivotal dialogue in that first counseling session word for word.

"Christy, you became a Christian, a believer, at a young age, correct?"

"Yes. I accepted Christ as my Savior at Vacation Bible School when I was eight."

"Christy, do you need a Savior?"

"Of course I do."

"And what is it you need to be saved from?"

"I need to be saved from sin so that I may spend eternity in heaven with Him."

"Well, will you let Him save you from this?"

"From what?"

"From this sin."

"What is this sin?"

"Relational idolatry."

When her counselor used the term *idolatry* in reference to Christy, she was shocked because she knew idolatry was a sin. It became clear to Christy she was worshiping people over God. The approval and security of others had become more important to her than God's approval and security.

What I have seen, both in my own life and in the lives of other believers who are on the road to freedom, is that God often has to shock us to awaken us. He may use friends, He may use His Word, or He may use suffering. He'll do whatever it takes to show us the tumors growing in our hearts because His love for us is intense.

The term "relational idolatry" *did* awaken Christy, for deep in her heart she loved God and did not want to be an idolater. Now she had a specific sin she could present to the Lord for His forgiveness and confess to Him the guilt and shame she felt for having her affections misplaced. She wanted to be set free from the misery that she kept experiencing. So she was willing to do whatever it took, no matter how painful.

Christy's response reminds me of Eustace, the boy in *The Voyage of the* Dawn Treader by C. S. Lewis whose love of approval and power had turned him into a dragon. When Aslan, the lion who represents Jesus, said, "You will have to let me undress you," Eustace thought:

> I was afraid of his claws, I can tell you, but I was pretty nearly desperate now. So I just lay flat down on my back to let him do it.
>
> That very first tear he made was so deep that I thought it had gone right into my heart. And when he began pulling the skin off, it hurt worse than anything I'd ever felt. The only thing that made me able to bear it was just the pleasure of feeling the stuff peel off.[13]

Christy's counselor told her she needed a period of separation from Brooke and needed to learn how to let Jesus be what no friend could ever be. Only then would her friendships become healthy. Christy obeyed, explained to Brooke that she needed to get healthy, and then spent a year in counseling and in immersing herself in books and studies about relational idolatry. She began to practice setting her affections on Jesus, going to Him in her mind throughout the day—the way she used to do with a friend.

Christy did get healthy, and so have her friendships. She says now, "It feels so good to be free. And so good to truly be experiencing more of the presence of the Lord."

An evidence of Christy's healing occurred to me while we were having lunch in an airport together and she got a call from Brooke. Brooke, who now lives in another state, was in Kansas City and hoping to see Christy. Christy explained she wasn't there and would miss her. Though disappointed that she would miss her friend's visit, Christy was not devastated. Their friendship was a gift, not a god.

When Christy hung up, we talked about our particular idols and how they both had been destructive to relationships. I told her again how sorry I was about my manipulative ways when she had worked for me, and she held up her hand, letting me know that was in the past, forgiven, over. I'm thankful for her grace.

I think the story of the blind man and how at first he saw people as "walking trees" also represents how our idols can keep us from seeing people as Jesus would have us see them. Instead of seeing others with hurts and needs, we use them, seeing them as a way to meet our own needs.

People in the world "bite and devour one another" (Galatians 5:15) because their idols dominate them, but we are to put off that way of life and put on Christ. I was devouring my administrative assistants. And as Christy confesses: "I wasn't addicted to a substance or running to food for comfort; I was feasting on people." When the Stonecutter moves in and crushes our idols, our relationships are transformed. We see people, not as "walking trees," but as Jesus sees them. A new sweetness comes into our relationships with everyone. What I see in Christy is a growing radiance and conformity to Christ— a woman who is being set free.

Recently Christy traveled with me to Bemidji, Minnesota, to the deep woods, to the place where they tell the tall Paul Bunyan tales. We drove by a giant statue of Babe, Paul Bunyan's blue ox—a statue that eerily reminded us of the Israelites' golden calf. We talked about that story in Exodus and how, in the past, we were mystified at how God's people, because they were impatient for Moses to return from the mountain, could actually melt their jewelry, make a calf of gold, and then *worship* it. Such blasphemy to the God who had been so good to them! And yet we are just as foolish, just as blind, if we do not see that soul idolatry is also blasphemous to the God who died for us.

Soul Idolatry: Excludes Men Out of Heaven

The above chilling title is from David Clarkson, who lived in the 1600s. Clarkson defines two kinds of idolatry, one as perilous as the other.

1. Open, outward idolatry: When men, out of a religious respect, bow to, or prostrate themselves before anything besides God. . . .
2. Secret and soul idolatry: When the mind and heart is set on anything more than God; when anything is more valued than God, more trusted . . . more loved.[14]

Once you begin to understand soul idolatry, you see it everywhere in Scripture. We can make our belly our god (Philippians 3:19). The love of money can cause us to wander from the faith and plunge us into destruction (1 Timothy 6:9–10). We can make family our god and be unworthy of Christ (Matthew 10:37). We can trust in friends instead of God and be like a shrub in the desert (Jeremiah 17:5–6). God tells us over and over again how serious this is. Clarkson—drawing upon the statement in Ephesians 5:5 that an idolater "has no inheritance in the kingdom of Christ and God"—writes, "'Secret idolaters' shall have no inheritance in the kingdom of God. Soul idolatry will exclude men out of heaven as well as open idolatry. He who serves his lusts is as incapable of entering heaven, as he who worships idols of wood or stone!"[15]

If you truly know the Lord, then the promise is that "he who began a good work in you will bring it to completion at the day of Jesus Christ" (Philippians 1:6). But if your soul is continually set on other things, then it is prudent to question whether you do know Him, even if you can repeat correct doctrine or went forward at an altar call.

We should long to be free of soul idolatry, not only to give us assurance that we are, indeed, God's, but to cooperate with the process so that we can experience the intimacy and life God longs for us to have right now.

What intrigues me, and what I have pondered, prayed, and dialogued about with sisters of depth, is why two believers with the same problem can hear the same message on idols of the heart and yet one is set free and the other remains chained.

Recently my friend Leslie Vernick, a Christian counselor who has gained respect among her peers, came to my cabin for a long weekend and we talked about this dilemma. When Leslie received her training at Westminster Theological Seminary through the Christian Counseling and Educational Foundation, she was taught how important it was to help clients see their idols if they were to get free.[16] I want to share with you what I learned in our time together that was pivotal in shedding light on the dark waters of our souls.

I want you to be in the group that is set free.

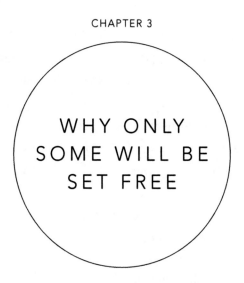

CHAPTER 3

WHY ONLY SOME WILL BE SET FREE

Why do some persons "find" God in a way that others do not? . . . I venture to suggest that the one vital quality which they had in common was spiritual receptivity. . . . They had spiritual awareness and they went on to cultivate it until it became the biggest thing in their lives.

—A. W. Tozer, *The Pursuit of God*

I had just finished speaking at a retreat with an author I respect when she invited me to come to an exclusive retreat for Christian women authors. She told me: "You'll meet the most wonderful women, you'll be in balmy southern Texas in January, and it's by invitation only. Dee, we want you!" My approval idol sat up and smiled—I had made it into a select sorority! The last thing my friend said before she left the room was "Please come,

Dee! You'll love it!" Then she peeked back in the door with an afterthought: "Oh, and it will be great for your health!"

That should have been a clue, but it wasn't. I signed up, flew to Texas, and piled in the van bound for the ranch with many well-known authors. I recognized some who had books on the *New York Times* bestseller list and felt intimidated. (Now my approval idol was cowering. I thought: *Will these women respect me and want to be with me?*)

When we arrived at the ranch, the coordinator, Carole, said, "Go up, unpack, come on down, and line up to get weighed." She pointed to a shining silver scale in the foyer. I froze.

What? Get weighed? What is this?

Suddenly my friend's parting words came back to me. "Oh, it will be great for your health!" I thought, *Oh no, this is by invitation only to* fat *authors*.

THE FAT GIRLS' CAMP

The author retreat wasn't really a "Fat Girls' Camp," but torturous memories from my teens kept haunting me. When I was fifteen, I weighed 120 pounds—ten pounds over where Mother thought I should be. She said, "Let's nip this in the bud." Well-intentioned, she sent me to Camp Seascape, a six-week summer camp on Cape Cod for obese Jewish girls. (I do not know how my mother found it or got me in, since I was neither obese nor Jewish.) When my parents filled out the application, they had to say which side of the family had a tendency toward obesity. They got hysterical, each pointing to the other's family and denying any tendency in their own.

I didn't think it was funny at all.

The camp lived up to my nightmares. I felt shame that I had to be there. I felt ostracized by both the heavy campers and the model thin trainers. I had no friends. The trainers made us swim laps in the icy waters of Nantucket Sound, telling us it would melt our fat. I saw them laughing as they sat on their lawn chairs, watching us plow through the chilling waves.

It took me the whole six weeks to lose my ten pounds, whereas most girls lost forty to seventy pounds. Each weekly weigh-in felt like a failure.

I don't think my mother should have sent me there or that my dad should have gone along with it. But I understand better now, because I see idols—as Paul did when he traveled to Athens—under everything, motivating everyone's choices. My mother was an exceptionally beautiful woman and she wanted her daughters to be beautiful as well. She also was impacted, as we all are, by cultural and gender idols. In America, in her generation and in ours, a huge idol for women is physical beauty. We are continually pressured to look striking, slim, and sexy. It's why eating disorders are rampant and why women's magazines are filled, not with articles to stimulate the mind, but with glossy pages on how to attain this idol of feminine beauty. We all crave it to a degree and can hate ourselves when we look fat, frumpy, or old.

(In biblical days, the idol for women was different. That culture valued family, and in particular, the bearing of sons. Again and again we see the desperation of barren biblical women and the scorn heaped upon them. They craved children and many hated themselves if they could not have them.)

My parents were wonderful, but when they failed, I believe the root cause was idolatry. My mother found her identity in beauty and my father worshiped my mother. Every day he said, "She's the best thing that ever happened to me." Idols drive us to make foolish choices—like sending your not-so-fat daughter to a fat girls' camp.

But, thank God, this week in Texas was not that at all. It was for spiritual, emotional, *and* physical health. Most of the authors were slender and welcomed a week of healthy eating and exercise after the holidays. In addition to biking, hiking, and calisthenics in the barn, there was worship, morning and evening devotions, and plenty of time on the porch to form wonderful friendships with women who understood the joys and trials of the writing life.

One of the women I felt particularly drawn to was Leslie Vernick. When she led us in devotions, she told us of a silent retreat she had gone on to draw closer to God. For five days she was alone with God. No cell phone, no computer, no iPod, no conversation with friends, no books—only her Bible and a notebook, a sparse room, and the great outdoors. I wondered, *Could I do that?* And more searchingly, I thought, *Would I want to do that?* She talked about how challenging it was for her and how it gave her insight into the darkness of her soul.

I thought, *I think the waters of my soul are darker than hers!* I was drawn to Leslie, wanting to be a woman like her, a woman who desired God first and foremost. I was pleased when she sought me out, and we began to share our hearts as we wrapped up in blankets and rocked in great Adirondack rockers on the porch. I took a risk and asked her if she'd consider coming to my cabin in Wisconsin, and she said, "Absolutely!" Then she followed up, wanting to get it on our calendars. A friendship was born.

AS IRON SHARPENS IRON

October arrived and so did Leslie. We were graced with perfect autumn weather, temperatures in the sixties, the trees at their peak, crimson and gold branches reaching into the bright blue sky—mirrored again on the waters of Green Bay. Leslie and I are both introverts who need our alone time in the morning, but then, in the afternoon, we were ready to come together to hike or bike through God's wondrous world and talk about the things that matter most. Leslie said, "We're a good friendship fit," and I smiled in happy agreement.

On one of the days we were together, we had biked (Leslie pushing me to do ten miles through the Wisconsin woods), then showered and rewarded our hungry selves with a supper of pumpkin soup, steaming freshly made bread, and broiled whitefish at an outdoor café in Fish Creek. The weather was warm enough to eat outside yet brisk enough for sweaters. What is better than breaking bread with a friend, sharing your souls, and experiencing the quickening that comes as the sparks fly back and forth? We both, as authors, had entered the blogging world and were seeing how interacting with our readers can bear fruit. Leslie answers a weekly counseling question on her blog, and I post a weekly Bible study.

I said, "Because you are a counselor, you can see firsthand which clients change and which do not. But for me, I didn't have that window until I entered the blogging world. Right now I'm testing the Bible study that will go with *Idol Lies*. Some people are changing dramatically, naming their idols, and turning to God. Others are not. Some are faithful, and others begin eagerly but drop out quickly. What do you think makes the difference?"

Leslie didn't hesitate. She quoted A. W. Tozer, the words tumbling out of the overflow of her heart: "True spirituality manifests itself in certain dominant desires. These ever-present deep-seated wants are sufficiently powerful to motivate and control a life."[17]

"And what are those desires?"

"To pursue God, to glorify God—even if it means that the person herself will suffer temporary dishonor or loss."

"Hmmm. And to want God for Him instead of what He can give us?"

"Yes."

"And what about those who don't really want God?"

"They're still in the grasp of their idols."

"So they are not delivered from the power of sin."

"Right."

I thought of how clearly I had seen that with the women on my blog. I told Leslie: "Last January I posted a study to help women keep their New Year's resolutions. I warned them it wouldn't be an easy fix, because we were going to attack the deep idols to get to the root. There were so many women who signed up who had the resolution to lose weight. It felt overcrowded—like a Weight Watchers meeting the first week after New Year's. By late or even mid-January, most of them had disappeared."

She nodded. She had seen the same thing in her practice. Some believers come for what they can get quickly, but they certainly don't want heart surgery.

I pondered.

We ate our pear and goat cheese salads quietly. I realized that there could be many reasons women dropped out. I smiled, thinking of Cyndi, whom I've come to love for her painful honesty. She dropped out, then came back confessing that she realized she had dropped out because of *soul* idolatry. She wasn't getting enough affirmation from us. She said, "I'd get up in the morning running to my computer for kind words from all of you instead of going to my sweet Savior to let Him fill me up." She came back in humble repentance, this time desiring to desire God.

Then I thought about the women who stayed and had experienced radical change. I told Leslie about Rebecca.

"When Rebecca came on, she did so because she was missing the intimacy she once had had with Jesus. She talked about a wall between her and God. Someone told her she thought my study would help her, but when she saw it was on idolatry, she didn't think that was her problem. When I confessed my heart idols, Rebecca began to wonder if she had them too. She knew she was depressed but blamed her stressful life. She has four sons under twelve, two on the autism spectrum, and a husband who works eighty hours a week. Yet slowly she began to see that she was not running to God but to a comfort idol, which manifested itself in overeating in front of the news at night."

"Both of those behaviors can suck you in. Addictive."

"As her weight ballooned, so did her depression."

"They fed each other."

"Mm-hmm." I thought about how that could happen in my own life. "Rebecca was *so* transparent on the blog. She asked, 'If I give up overeating at night, will God just let me sit in my pain?'"

"That's great," Leslie said. "She expressed what so many women must have been thinking but were hesitant to express."

"Yes! Even me. With my control idol, I often ask: *Can I trust God to be the One in control? What if I don't like how He does things?*"

"What happened with Rebecca?"

"We looked at pictures from the prophets that talk about God loving us like a Bridegroom, of Him dancing over us with singing. Rebecca began to take steps of faith. Not only has she been freed from being overweight and depressed, but she'll often come on and describe the intimacy she is now sensing with Jesus. She wrote: 'Intimacy with Him is like a stream, and I don't like the rocks that get in the way of the flow.'"

Leslie's eyes filled.

"Leslie," I said, "I love that desire for intimacy with God in you. That's what first attracted me to you at the Fat Girls' Camp."

"Don't call it that! You know it wasn't."

"Easy for skinny you to say. Your mother never traumatized you."

We gave the waitress our credit cards and asked her to split the bill down the middle. (Even though Leslie had wine and *I* didn't. *I* have to watch my weight.)

On the drive home I told Leslie how Rebecca is spotting other idols. Rebecca is a tall, gorgeous woman with an incredible voice, yet she was absolutely paralyzed with fear when asked to sing at church. In fact, the week before she was scheduled to sing a solo at church, she started posting pictures of the enormous sanctuary on her Facebook page so we could empathize with her fear.

Leslie said, "When I started speaking in public, my legs literally shook. I understood that expression 'weak knees.' I had to take my soul in hand. When I looked at the crowd, I said to myself, *You are not my life—Christ is my life.*"

"That's exactly what Rebecca did. The morning before she sang she told herself that even if she went off key, even if she forgot all the words, even if she completely flopped in front of her church—Christ was still her life. He came to her. His Spirit told her to sing just for Him."

"And?"

"It was amazing. Truly anointed. She posted the video on the blog and we were all blown away. God was so glorified. You could really see she was singing for Him."

When we try to use God to get what *we* want but we don't really want Him, we will not succeed for long. We may have temporary success—losing weight for a high school reunion, controlling our temper so we don't lose a client, or staying in a Bible study as long as people are affirming us. But if we don't really want God, our idols will continue to grow, taking over our souls like a cancer. If our dominant desire is for God, transformation will happen. Jeremiah tells us, "If you wanted to return to me, you could. You could throw away your detestable idols and stray no more" (Jeremiah 4:1, NLT). Do you see? If our deepest desire is for God, we will want to release the idols that are blocking our intimacy with Him. And then He may give us back the gifts we were abusing—the friendship, the food, the money—and we will turn to them, not as gods, but as ways to glorify Him.

IDOL LIES

When Leslie and I returned to the cabin, the sun was sinking into the flat-calm bay, and Leslie wanted to kayak. (I was beginning to figure out how she stayed so thin.) We pushed our kayaks into the bay to glide through the golden water, the sun slipping down behind us. The little village of Ephraim twinkled ahead—white lights in the cabins and shops, two gleaming white church steeples poking high above the cedar bluffs. The sky was darkening, and we had no lights of our own. "We'd better turn back," I said. We dipped our paddles in on just one side, long strokes, and our kayaks turned toward the sky where the sun had disappeared. *Glory.* Crimson had flooded the heavens and the bay.

Leslie said, "I feel like we're headed toward heaven."

We paddled in silence, breathing in His beauty.

I thought about how God's glory is everywhere, which is why we are told that people are "without excuse" (Romans 1:20). They know God, yet they refuse to glorify Him. They suppress the truth so they can chase after their idols. I was eager to take up the conversation with Leslie but didn't want to break the silence of slipping through the bay, spread with scarlet splendor. So I waited until we had pulled the kayaks on shore and were in our pajamas. We warmed ourselves before the crackling fire with mugs of spiced tea.

"As we were kayaking, I kept thinking of Romans 1."

"Yes. God's glory is everywhere, yet we exchange the truth for a lie, worshiping the created thing instead of the Creator."

I stood up and took a book from the shelf, handing it to Leslie. It was *Washed and Waiting* by Wesley Hill, a memoir of what it is like to live as a celibate gay man. "I loved the honesty of this memoir. He admits he has not been completely delivered from his sexual desires, yet because of his love for God and his faith in His Word, he is living a celibate life. He says his life has been filled with temptation but *also* with power and joy. My takeaway from it is that he was able to refute the lie that had brought down so many of his friends in the gay and lesbian community—that if they denied their longings, they would live 'a lesser life.' He quotes C. S. Lewis, saying that it's the sexually active homosexual who has the lesser life."

"This isn't a truth just for people who are gay."

"Exactly! Because Paul illustrates this principle with the example of practicing same-sex passion, my sinful heart narrowed the principle to that application only, instead of seeing that the principle applies to all kinds of idol temptations, including mine! So many of the struggles that Hill faced, I also face. As a youngish widow, I face grief, loneliness, and sexual temptation and am continually living with my own brokenness. There *is* pain that cannot be denied and may not be completely removed until heaven. Continually I must choose between allowing God to comfort me or creating my own comfort in ways that hurt me and my relationship with Him."

"This is a truth for all of us. The mother of a child with special needs, the woman who longs to be married and is not—any of us can deal with pain in destructive ways. If our only goal in life is to avoid pain, then the downward spiral described in Romans 1—of God giving us over to a darkened mind and the grasp of our idols—can happen to any of us. We need to see the lie we have exchanged for the truth."

I thought about how when I exaggerate to make myself look better in the eyes of others, I am bowing down to approval. When I overeat, I'm bowing down to comfort. When it is too important to me to be a successful Christian wife, mother, or author, it is because my identity is in those things and not in Christ. I, too, move into that downward spiral, away from God and toward my crouching idols.

Then I thought about the biography I'd read the summer before of John Newton, the slave trader who repented and went on to write the lyrics for the hymn "Amazing Grace." I'd been surprised that it took him so long to wake up to the realization that kidnapping Africans was sin.

I told Leslie about it. "Though John Newton was a proclaiming Christian, for decades he could not see his sin. He even prayed God would help him catch slaves. And in a letter he wrote to his wife, Polly, from his slave-trading boat he said, 'I feel I've been shut up with almost as many unclean creatures as Noah was, and in a much smaller ark.'"[18]

"That's a perfect example for your book, Dee. Newton exchanged the truth of God for a lie—the lie that Africans were not really people. Believing that lie helped him pursue his idols of power and money."

I asked Leslie to give me an everyday example of this from her life.

"I'm in line at the store, in a hurry, and the clerk is slow. I feel myself getting angry, irritated. That's the signal from my body that my idol is operating, that I am worshiping something besides God, that I am exchanging the truth of God for a lie."

"So what do you do?"

"I ask myself what the idol is. In this case it is myself, my agenda, my schedule."

"Then what?"

"First, confess. I am not more important than this clerk. I am not loving her as God does. Then I must repent, asking Him to help me turn and love this clerk. I want to worship the Creator instead of the idol of myself and my own agenda."

Leslie's illustration shows how change must embrace both parts of the gospel: repentance and faith. She had to see her sin and repent but then also move toward the clerk in love, if only in her own thought life.

So the first part of the gospel helps us see our sin and the second part helps us move forward in faith, to trust God. Jack Miller's definition of the gospel is helpful:

A. We are more sinful than we could ever imagine (for Christ had to die).

B. We are more loved than we ever dared dream (for He *did* die).[19]

Part A should make us ever aware of our depravity and our tendency to deceive ourselves. When Leslie's body language revealed to her that something was wrong, she looked for the lie she had believed and the idol she was embracing and she repented. Part B gives us the confidence that if we move forward in faith God will be there for us, for we are so loved that He *did* die for us. Therefore, Leslie could trust that if she let go of her agenda and stopped stewing over the clerk's slowness, she would still get done what God wanted her to do. She could freely give the clerk the love and grace God wanted her to give.

If our dominant desire is for God, then daily we will experience the combustion cycle of repentance (away from the idol and his lies) and faith (toward God and His truth). Once we understand this combustion cycle and submit to it, our growth will accelerate dramatically.

REPENTANCE *AND* FAITH

I was going to be with a relative over the holidays with whom I tend to clash. Honestly, I want to control him. I want to change his thinking. I want him to be different.

I want him to be like me.

It's my control idol. I often find manipulative thoughts rising in me, wanting to zing him with a remark about what I see as warped theology or behavior. This time we were going to be together for three days, and I wondered if I would make it. I asked my youngest daughter to pray for me. She said: "Mom, it isn't enough to stop being mean—you have to really love him."

"I just wanted prayer."

She unsuccessfully suppressed a smile.

"You're right," I conceded.

Just as the thief must stop stealing and start working for a living, so the mean person must stop cutting down and start building up (Ephesians 4:28–29).

Stop, start.

Repentance, faith.

I was amazed at how much Annie's advice helped me with this relative. When an unkind or manipulative thought came to me, I didn't just *not* say it; I asked God to help me say something kind and true. And He did. I made an effort to have the special foods I know this relative likes, and I read an essay he'd written and expressed appreciation for its strong points. I began to see him differently. I realized that I had been building up a stereotype of him in my mind instead of seeing him as a person with hurts and needs. I had believed a lie.

He saw me differently too. But then, I *was* different! When he left, he hugged me sincerely and said, "It's been really good to be with you."

He's never said that before.

My relationships are changing. Instead of seeing people as "walking trees," I am seeing them more and more as God does. He loves them, sees their hurts, and knows their vulnerability to idolatry, but He also sees the beautiful beings they could become. The new grace in my heart flows like a healing stream, bringing life to others and to myself. People find more life than they used to by being with me, I am experiencing more of the amazing presence of God, and even the stiff neck that used to plague me has disappeared. This is all of Christ.

God is passionate for us, so He will do whatever it takes to awaken us to the danger we are in and stop us. He uses some shocking metaphors in His Word to get our attention. He'll also shake our world to get our attention. His purposes are for our good and for His glory. He wants to rescue us from the downward spiral so that we turn and run into the safety of His arms.

I pray that is where you want to go. I pray your dominant desire is for God. Then, indeed, you will be set free.

PART 2

Shafts of Light

He uncovers the deeps out of darkness

and brings deep darkness to light.

———

Job 12:22

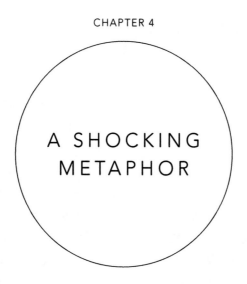

CHAPTER 4

A SHOCKING METAPHOR

It is a bold and creative stroke by which God, instead of banning sexual imagery from religion, rescues and raises it to portray the ardent love and fidelity which are the essence of His covenant.

—Derek Kidner, *The Message of Hosea*

I was seated on the airplane, flying from Atlanta to Milwaukee, absorbed in Jerry Bridges's book *Respectable Sins*, letting its truth wash over my idolatrous soul. So often, Bridges says, we as believers downplay sins like selfishness, gossip, gluttony, and pride—all the time patting ourselves on the back because we aren't murderers or adulterers. He gave an example of a pastor who finally canceled the men's prayer meeting because the men were praying only about the community's sins and never seeing and confessing the darkness in their own souls.

I was aware that the man seated next to me was covertly trying to see what I was reading. Finally he said, "That's a great title."

I smiled, wondering if he might be a brother in the Lord.

Then he said: "Yep! I really like that! There *are* respectable sins."

(I wish I had asked him what those might be!)

It's so easy to think of our own sins as being "respectable." I certainly justified my manipulative ways for years, blind to the boulder in my heart. Sins like complaining, ignoring the enormous needs in Third World countries, or withdrawing behind a wall instead of truly forgiving may feel "respectable" to us, but they don't to God. They wound Him and harden our own hearts.

God knows us. He knows how we justify our sins, how we close our eyes to our stones, and how badly we need to be awakened. So He uses an absolutely shocking analogy to bring us to our senses.

He tells us we are guilty of adultery.

What?

Yes.

When we practice soul idolatry by running to things other than God to meet our needs, we betray our one true Lover. God uses this metaphor to help us see both a negative truth and a positive truth:

1. The negative: Sin is not breaking rules but breaking God's heart.

2. The positive: He will come to us, confide in us, and fill us with His presence when we truly turn away from our false lovers and run to Him.

THE NEGATIVE: BREAKING GOD'S HEART

Recently when I was staying at a hotel on Chicago's Magnificent Mile, a couple in the room on the other side of the wall was having a marital quarrel. The issue seemed to be infidelity. There was shouting, name-calling, and sobbing—all oozing through the cracks of the locked door separating their room from mine.

I felt I should not be there. There was no way I could not hear. I also realized an argument like this could last into the wee small hours of the morning, so I called and asked the front desk for another room, which they quickly gave me. As I packed my bag to move to another floor, I thought of how like the book of Hosea this couple sounded.

Isaiah, Jeremiah, and Ezekiel all liken God's people to an unfaithful wife who goes after her lovers. But it is the little book of Hosea that paints a life-sized mural of an unfaithful wife and a brokenhearted husband from beginning to end. Accusations, defenses, and palpable pain seep through the pages.

God asks Hosea to marry Gomer, a woman known for her promiscuity, a woman who would be repeatedly unfaithful to him. God wants His people to watch Hosea, to see that despite Hosea's long-suffering faithfulness, his wife breaks his heart over and over again. When we run to other things to fill the emptiness in our hearts, when we "get in bed" with other lovers, we break God's heart.

Why does Gomer run after her lovers? She says:

> I will go after my lovers,
>> who give me my bread and my water,
>> my wool and my flax, my oil and my drink.
>
> (Hosea 2:5)

When we turn to sin, whatever it is—lying, gossiping, sexual immorality—we are doing it because we are trying to solve a problem. We do not think God can help us with this problem. When I manipulated, it was because I did not trust God to be in control. When Christy clung too tightly to her friend, it was because she did not trust God to be her security. When Rebecca overate, it was because she feared that God would let her sit in her pain. So, like Gomer, we run to lovers whom we think *really* help us. But they won't—that's the idol lie. They will destroy us.

And we break God's heart, just as Gomer breaks Hosea's heart.

When a believer thinks, *I have to fudge a little in filling out my taxes because money is tight,* he doesn't just hurt himself by running to dishonesty, he breaks God's heart. Why? Because God longs to be his Provider, his Jehovah-Jireh.

When a believer thinks, *I can't forgive this wretched person* and clings to a grudge, she doesn't just hurt herself. She is grieving the One who laid down His life for her when she too was undeserving.

What I am seeing in my life is that I fall into the trap of wanting Jesus *plus* something else—for my children to love me well, for my writing to be blessed, for suffering to be removed from my life. But I want to be content with God alone and to trust that He knows best when He gives or withholds earthly blessings. I do not want to be the kind of woman who married a man for what he could give her and then runs to other lovers when she does not get what she wants from him.

Gomer keeps running to her false lovers, thinking they are the ones who *really* help her. Listen to Hosea's brokenhearted cries:

> She did not know
>   that it was I who gave her
>   the grain, the wine, and the oil
> and who lavished on her silver and gold.
>
> (Hosea 2:8)

And:

> "[She] went after her lovers,
> and forgot me," declares the LORD.
>
> (verse 13)

We are like Gomer. We forget the Lord, running to the lovers we think can give us what we need. This is betrayal. This is adultery. As Philip Yancey writes, "The prophets proclaim loud and clear how God feels: he loves us. Of the ancient gods, Israel's God alone stooped to admit love for the flawed, two-legged creatures who roam this planet. God's cries of pain and anger are the cries of a wounded lover, distressed over our lack of response."[20]

Recently, when I was ministering in the Texas prisons, I met a radiant woman I'll call Ellen, who was an orthodontist before she was imprisoned. Ellen was halfway through her twenty-year sentence. After talking to her, I thought, *You are lovely. If you lived in my town, I would pursue you as a friend. You have a depth, a love, and a radiance that comes only from Him.*

Later, when I was with my friend who is in charge of this prison ministry in Texas, I asked her what Ellen had done to receive such a long sentence. I was told that she had murdered her husband.

"Why?"

"Her daughter told her he was being unfaithful and named the hotel where he was with his mistress. Ellen drove to the hotel and saw him coming out with a beautiful woman, opening the door of her car and helping her in. Rage took over and she ran him down with her Mercedes."

A part of me empathized with how a woman could snap under such a betrayal. Ellen had made lifelong vows to her husband, loved him, made herself naked and vulnerable with him . . . and yet he had treated all that as if it meant nothing. Even God seems to understand how marital betrayal produces white rage, for He says in Proverbs, "He who commits adultery lacks sense. . . . For jealousy makes a man furious, and he will not spare when he takes revenge" (Proverbs 6:32–34). Of course we are not to take revenge—that belongs only to God. It was a dreadful sin for Ellen to murder her husband. She knows that, is walking in true repentance, and is being transformed by the power of God.

As I was thinking about Ellen's husband and his unfaithfulness, I thought: *That is what I have done to Christ. I have been unfaithful to Him and have broken His heart. I deserve to die for what I have done. I deserve to be "run down" by His Mercedes. Yet that is not how He responded. He was "run down" for me. He died in my place.*

Amazing love. How can it be?

Paying attention to the negative side of this metaphor can awaken us, helping us to see that our sins are not respectable at all, but grievous. But we can be so thankful that God doesn't just convict us with the negative side of this metaphor. Rather, He encourages us with the positive side—His amazing love, His great forgiveness, and His tenderness toward us, His unfaithful bride.

THE POSITIVE: INTIMACY WITH THE LOVER OF OUR SOULS

I have found that believers have an easier time accepting the negative side of the metaphor of adultery than the positive side. In part that is due to poor teaching on these intimate passages, but it is also because Satan, the father of lies, whispers to us: *Do you really think God could love someone like you?* The enemy's goal is to get us to doubt God's deep love for us so that we will fear letting go of our false lovers, so that we will continue to turn to our idols for elusive satisfaction.

Recently there was an article in *Christianity Today* titled "Disappointed with Intimacy." The writer of the article compared the Church's hype that we could experience sustainable intimacy with God to the hype on the back of a cereal box for a baking soda rocket. As a little boy, he ordered it with great expectations and was profoundly disappointed when it fizzled, swirling slowly to the bottom of the tub.[21] I was thankful that two months later *Christianity Today* published some strong rebuttals to this article, including a letter from me:

> I know that great waves of spiritual intimacy may never happen as they did to Pascal, Moody, and Spurgeon. But what is this quiet stream of inextinguishable joy if not the presence of my Lord? When I am still and sense his wisdom, or when a verse quickens me, is this not dialogue? And when a believer puts her arm around me and comforts me over the loss of my husband, is this not the touch of Christ? What is this if not intimacy? This is not the disappointment of a baking-soda rocket—this is what sustains me.[22]

Most of the time the unquenched presence of the Lord is like a quiet stream, not the crest of a wave. But it *can* be an overwhelming wave. The believers I mentioned in my letter tell of moments so passionate that some asked God to stay His hand. Blaise Pascal, the brilliant mathematician and philosopher, encountered the living God one night, and as happened for Isaiah, Pascal seemed to unravel. Pascal recorded what happened on a piece of parchment and sewed it into the lining of his coat, transferring it whenever the coat wore out, so he would never be without it:

From about half-past ten in the evening until
     about half-past twelve
... FIRE
... God of Abraham, the God of Isaac,
     the God of Jacob,
and not of the philosophers and savants.
Certitude. Certitude.
Feeling. Joy. Peace.[23]   ♠

For most of us, this kind of experience may never happen, or if it ever does, we should count ourselves richly blessed. It is what John Donne prayed for in his sonnet XIV, "Batter My Heart Three-Person'd God," when at the close he wrote:

Take me to You, imprison me, for I,
Except You enthrall me, never shall be free;
Nor ever chaste, except You ravish me.

I know this metaphor is shocking. Unbelievers simply cannot understand it. When agnostic Carolyn Weber began classes at Oxford, she was asked to write an essay on Donne's sonnet. She wrote what she thought was "a brilliant analysis of the domination of rape imagery in the poem" and the threat of male domination to maternal power. She thought herself "quite clever" but wanted to get her professor's take before her grade was finalized. To her astonishment, he told her point-blank that she had completely missed the point. He tried to explain that unless we sense God's love—His "ravishing" of us—we will fail to submit to Him and life will be futile. He told her she should use her time at Oxford to learn to discern the false from the true. Then he strode away.[24]

Huh? She had missed the point?

Yes.

But it isn't just unbelievers who have failed to see. Many believers have trouble grasping the positive side of this metaphor. In part, it's because they do not understand what a metaphor looks like.

THE POWER OF METAPHOR

I would never dare to use a sexual metaphor as I do here, except that God does it repeatedly in the poets, the prophets, the parables, and Paul's letters. But please remember, this is a metaphor. For example, when Jesus wept over Jerusalem and said He wished He could gather her under His wings, we must not press the metaphor to ridiculous lengths but grasp what He is trying to communicate by comparing Himself to a mother hen. He cares deeply for His people and wishes He could gather them "under His wing," but they resist, skittering away like senseless chicks.

Basic hermeneutics (the art of interpreting Scripture) will tell you to interpret genre according to genre, otherwise you risk *misinterpreting* it. We must understand that metaphors are a figure of speech, meant to convey a central concept.

Metaphors can slip past our natural defenses and help us understand the heart of God. In *The Language of Love*, Gary Smalley and John Trent explain that though you may explain a truth again and again to others, they are much more likely to finally understand when a word picture is used. And this intimate metaphor of sexuality, used repeatedly in Scripture, is rich, nuanced, and powerful.

When Scripture uses the sexual metaphor, it certainly doesn't mean we are engaging in a sexual act with God, like some ancient and modern cults say. (I feel foolish even saying this, but I know I must because of the emails and letters I received after Kathy Troccoli and I wrote our trilogy on *Falling in Love with Jesus*.) It means that as we increase in our love, trust, and intimacy with the Almighty, as we willingly put ourselves "in His arms," our lives will have a fruitfulness that can come only when we yield to the Spirit of God. This is a metaphor, and it is an important one—for women and for men.

When I was on Moody radio, I had an opportunity to interview Michael Card, a man whose songs reveal that he understands this important metaphor. I asked him how he, as a man, related to being the bride of Christ. He said first that he was glad there was a metaphor for which women had the advantage, because there are so many metaphors in Scripture in which men have the advantage. But he said he *could* relate, even though he was a man, explaining, "I don't think Scripture is going to give us a metaphor that the Holy Spirit cannot help us relate to. I don't ever want to say that there is a part of the Bible that is not for me or not for you. I hope I never become so sexualized that I can't see the meaning here."

What does it mean to become so sexualized that we miss the meaning of God's imagery? C. S. Lewis commented on our over-sexualized culture in *Mere Christianity*, observing how crowds will come to a nightclub to see a woman slowly undress. Lewis asked, would you not think a culture's appetite for food had gone awry if you could fill a whole theater just by bringing a covered plate out on stage and slowly lifting the lid so everyone could see a mutton chop or a bit of bacon?[25] We must wonder whether our culture has warped our minds so that we can no longer see the beauty of this intimate metaphor.

I asked Michael what this metaphor meant to him and he said, with passion, "That image of being the bride of Christ is such a powerful image—but you have to use your imagination. I can certainly relate through my relationship with my bride, Susan. Christ has reached out to me with His affection in the same way I have reached out to Susan Kepley, many years ago, asking her to become Susan Card. This metaphor shows us that tender part of Jesus, that romantic part, that cherishing of us."[26]

Cherished. Do you believe you are cherished? That's the point—and that's what we see again and again when the positive side of the metaphor appears. Isaiah, Jeremiah, and Ezekiel all have beautiful imagery of a loving Bridegroom cherishing His bride. And Zephaniah says:

> The LORD your God is in your midst,
>   a mighty one who will save;
> he will rejoice over you with gladness,
>   he will quiet you by his love;
> he will exult over you with loud singing.
>
> (Zephaniah 3:17)

But the most extended passages showing the positive side of this bridegroom metaphor occur in the poetry of the Bible—in the Psalms and the Song of Songs. Psalm 45 paints a picture of a mighty bridegroom coming forth from ivory palaces for his bride, who is glorious within her chamber. Likewise, when the "beloved" in the Song of Songs self-consciously protests, asking her "lover" not to gaze on her, for she is dark, he reassures her that he finds her beautiful, a "lily among thorns."

Up until the last century, believers saw the metaphorical level of the Song of Songs and not just the earthly level. But today many believers balk at the metaphorical level. I don't know if it is because we are so sexualized or because sex has become so polluted, but it is common for me to hear what one pastor expressed to me: "The Song of Songs can't relate to Christ, Dee, because it is too sexual."

I protested, referencing Charles Spurgeon: "How could this be called the Song of Songs if it was only about marriage? Marriage is a wonderful gift, but it can't be the best of the best. That honor belongs only to Christ." When godly men of the past such as Spurgeon, Hudson Taylor, and A. W. Tozer refer to the Song of Songs, they see not only the earthly level but also our relationship to Christ. A. W. Tozer tells us to follow hard after God and to say to our souls, "Arise, my love, my fair one, and come away" (Song of Songs 2:13, KJV).[27]

Could it be that by applying the Song of Songs *only* to earthly marriage we are missing its primary meaning? Song of Songs is a treasure, for though we see Jesus in every book of the Bible, it is in this book that we see His heart for us. And when we see His heart, we want to turn from our idols and run to Him.

We may find it hard to believe that God could see us as "glorious and pure," as being as "lily white," as having His banner of love waving over us, yet is this not the good news of the gospel? The positive side of this metaphor is meant to show us that we are indeed cleansed and accepted, beloved, and cherished—and the response our Bridegroom wants is not dutiful and dry religion but adoration, communion, and intimacy.

Ann Voskamp uses this poetic language of intimacy in *One Thousand Gifts*: "God lays down all His fullness into all the emptiness. I am in Him. He is in me. . . . Anywhere—in the kitchen scrubbing potatoes, in the arching cathedrals, in the spin of laundry and kids and washing toilets—anywhere I can have intimate communion with the Maker of heaven and earth. . . . The intercourse of soul with God is the very climax of joy."[28]

Not surprisingly, Voskamp's writing brought sharp attacks. One blogger said, "Run for your life." Another said, "This is what garners five stars from Amazon?" Yet, as thousands of other readers have discovered, it is this image of intimacy with God that takes us higher, making us realize that communion with God is truly possible.

So why do so many Christians stumble on this image? Just as those who have had an abusive father may struggle with the picture of God as Father, so those who have been exposed to a heap of sexual trash through the media may struggle with this metaphor of God as Spouse. And frankly, that is most of us. I remember when this metaphor came up during a small-group Bible study I was facilitating on live Moody radio and a young Australian participant cried out, "Oh, Dee—don't mix God and sex!"

First I responded that I understood how she felt, for it is hard to live in this world and not see sex as dirty. But God Himself pronounces the marriage bed to be good and honorable (Hebrews 13:4). It was His plan for a couple to be pure and faithful to one another, to renew their marriage covenant in a tangible way repeatedly through sexual intimacy. I told her we needed to reclaim what the world has stolen from our marriages and reclaim the metaphor for our spiritual lives as well, for *all* Scripture is profitable, including this oft-repeated metaphor. It's found not just in the poets and the prophets but throughout Scripture. In fact, the foundational verse about marriage, which talks about a husband and a wife becoming one flesh, begins in Genesis and is repeated five times throughout Scripture, finally culminating in Ephesians when Paul reveals that it isn't just about earthly marriage but points to a much more lasting mysterious marriage: "'For this reason a man will leave his father and mother and be united to his wife, and the two will become one flesh.' This is a profound mystery—but I am talking about Christ and the church" (Ephesians 5:31–32, NIV).

Pastor Tim Keller has boldly explained this metaphor to his New York congregation, saying that one day it will no longer be just a metaphor:

> The ecstasy and joy of sex is supposed to be a foretaste of the complete ecstasy and joy of total union with Christ. The moment we see Christ face to face, there will be a closure, and yet a complete openness. . . . We will be naked, yet so delighted in [our nakedness that] we will be unashamed. . . . The Lord God will look at us through Jesus and say, "I love you." . . . Great sex is a parable of the

Gospel—to be utterly accepted in spite of your sin, to be loved by the One you admire to the sky.[29]

Isn't that what we long for in our heart of hearts—to be known and yet to be loved? And we must not confine this metaphor just to sexual intimacy, for it is bigger than that, just as marriage is bigger than the sexual component. Paul says that when a wife respects and submits to her husband, she reflects the ultimate Bride, and when a husband cherishes and sacrifices for his wife, he reflects the ultimate Bridegroom. We begin to see the bigger picture.

I was blessed to have a husband who cherished me and sacrificed for me in countless little ways. He gave me foot rubs nearly every night, even when he was dying of cancer. He encouraged me to accept speaking engagements, even though he would need to be a solo parent on those weekends. He wore a wool cap and gloves to bed because I slept best in a cold bedroom snuggled next to him under a downy quilt. His love for me released a trust in me that made our marriage one of sweet communion. His dominant desire in our marriage was not for himself but for me. How like Christ.

Do you see? As wonderful as an earthly bridegroom might be, we have One who made the ultimate sacrifice. Jesus left paradise to come to earth and die in agony. Why? For us! That He might have us as His Bride! Can we not trust this love and allow it to release from us a reckless abandon? The negative side of the metaphor helps us to see our sin and repent, but we must see the positive side as well so we have the courage to move forward in faith and trust that Christ will meet us.

The passage I want us to look at in the next chapter, Jeremiah 2, is laden with positive and negative sexual images. So many women in our pilot studies said that Jeremiah 2, because it was so very shocking, jolted them awake. Finally they saw the truth about their idol lies and were set gloriously free.

Lily is one such woman. Let me tell you Lily's story and how God used Jeremiah 2 to rescue her from the downward spiral of her idolatry.

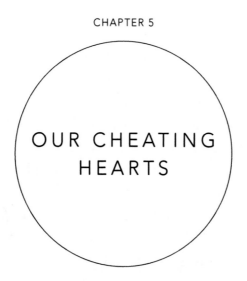

CHAPTER 5

OUR CHEATING HEARTS

Jeremiah paints God's Bride as a "restless wife to whom the bonds and burdens of true love were slavery, and the lure of the forbidden irresistible."

—Derek Kidner, *The Message of Jeremiah*

As children of God, we are not apt to pursue a path of outright rebellion. Instead, as we saw in the previous chapter, we engage in "respectable sins" to try to soothe our seething souls. For Lily, sinning respectably meant engaging in a fantasy that she was married to a believer who cherished her. She was trying to solve a problem, using what many would think was an acceptable solution. But any solution other than Christ destroys.

Lily was one of the first to participate in my online study on idolatry. When I asked the participants to identify one "stone" in their hearts, Lily said she saw a whole quarry, but she chose to identify her habit of fantasizing. She said:

> I don't know if I get bored with the same things every day, like cleaning bathrooms or doing laundry, but I tend to let my mind wander. I want to be really honest here. I make up a man in my mind, the ideal husband, someone who will really love me, and I fantasize about what that life would be like. . . . It is easier for me to behave as a Christian woman on the outside than it is to deal with my inner thought life.

It's natural to be sympathetic with Lily because she is married to an unbeliever who seems unappreciative of her. She works hard to make their home pleasant, but if she forgets to buy orange juice, her husband loses his temper. He often ridicules her faith in front of their children.

But here is the lie we must see, and which Lily eventually did. Idols, those malignant tumors, must be starved. God compares them to crouching beasts just waiting for an opportunity to devour us. (See Genesis 4:7) The deceptiveness of our idols can be seen in what happened to Lily—because at first, her habit of fantasizing did seem to give her happiness and relief.

THE LIE: YOUR IDOL
WILL RESCUE YOU

As Lily told our group online, about ten years earlier, before the birth of her third child, she and her husband became friends with another couple. The husband seemed to be everything

Lily's husband was not. Though she never did anything physically to act on her feelings, Lily thought about him constantly, engaging in her fantasies, feeding her idol. Whenever they went out with this couple, Lily made sure she looked her best. She lived for every opportunity to see this man.

"Fortunately," Lily told us, "God intervened, having the friendship simply go away—this couple just sort of disappeared from our lives."

But after her baby was born, Lily began to have health problems, as well as emotional problems such as panic attacks and depression. When Lily told me this, I thought what lying beasts our idols really are. I remember how stunned I was when my friend, Pastor Ed Longabaugh, told me, "Dee, idols always demand a sacrifice, a propitiation. They give you momentary relief and then *turn on you*, snarling, demanding payment." Lily's idol certainly turned on her. And yet, in the midst of her health problems, her despair, and her fears, her True Lover came to her, opening her eyes to the idol lie:

One night when I was home alone with the baby, I was on my knees praying, and I asked God, "Why can't I just be happy like I was a year ago?" I heard God's tender voice, in my mind, asking me, "What were you so happy about?" And I saw it. I saw how I had been making this man the source of my happiness. I saw that I was guilty of spiritual adultery. I saw my sin.

THE TRUTH: YOUR IDOL
WILL DESTROY YOU

The response "What were you so happy about?" to Lily's question to God is just like Jesus. He is a gentle Shepherd who asks questions, who longs to help us see ourselves as we are so that we might come to our senses and return to Him.

The sexual imagery in Jeremiah 2 jolted Lily awake. She saw that her "respectable sin" of fantasizing was not respectable at all, was not her friend, and was going to destroy her as surely as cocaine destroys its user. As we'll see, the language of Jeremiah 2 is intervention language—God pleads with Israel to stop worshiping false gods and giving themselves to other lovers. When God finally breaks through, the Israelites weep, for they realize they are addicted.

"I am seeing how my soul is churning," Lily said, "like many arms reaching for something to fill up the emptiness. Like the Israelites, I so often say, "'I must run after them [my idols]. I cannot help it!'"

I asked Lily to try to identify her "stone," the "sin beneath the sin," the idol that was producing the bad fruit of fantasizing, panic attacks, and depression. As so often happens for many of us, Lily saw two idols lurking in the waters of her soul: her longing for approval and her longing for security. She also realized that she had both of those in God.

She said, "How vividly God paints Himself as the broken-hearted husband who has been forsaken, who wondered what had happened to the bride who once was so in love with Him. Why had she left him for her lovers? What wrong had she found in Him?" This tender image helped Lily turn from her idol and toward her true Lover.

Recently Lily was watching the recent film adaptation of *Pride and Prejudice* with her daughter. In the closing scene, after Elizabeth and Mr. Darcy are married, Elizabeth asks him what he shall call her when he is just indescribably happy. He says, "I shall call you Mrs. Darcy." He keeps repeating this, "Mrs. Darcy, Mrs. Darcy . . ." and each time he says it, he kisses her tenderly on her forehead, her cheeks. . . . As she was watching this, Lily began feeling sad, thinking how tenderness was missing from her marriage. She thought, *Maybe I'll never know that kind of love*. In the past, the scene would have set her daydreaming about having that kind of man. But now she saw the lie and responded differently.

"I remembered the picture in Jeremiah 2 of God waiting for me—standing there with empty arms. I knew that Jesus wanted to give me that kind of tender, cherishing love. And, unlike my fantasies, Jesus is real."

Lily's stone is crumbling. Her one true Lover is coming to her, sustaining her. Her earthly marriage may continue to bring her pain. Often pain will not be removed before heaven. But Lily's heart is for holiness rather than happiness, to please God rather than to please herself. Just as Wesley Hill can live as a celibate homosexual, so can Lily live as a contented wife of an unbeliever. Both can let pain draw them nearer to God. Both can cling to the truth that this "slight momentary affliction" (though I know it doesn't feel that way) is preparing for them "an eternal weight of glory beyond all comparison" (2 Corinthians 4:17).

Let's consider the passage that was so pivotal in Lily's journey toward freedom.

THE DEVOTION OF YOUR YOUTH

Jeremiah 2 opens with a positive image, a picture of a bride so in love that she will follow her husband anywhere—a "whither thou goest, I will go" bride, who is content as long as she is with him.

> I remember the devotion of your youth,
>   your love as a bride,
> how you followed me in the wilderness,
>   in a land not sown.
>
> (Jeremiah 2:2)

This description reminds me of scenes from the television series *Little House on the Prairie,* which was based on the true story of Laura Ingalls Wilder's parents, Caroline and Charles. Caroline actually did follow her husband into the wilderness, into a land not sown. They lived in a little log house with winter winds whistling through the cracks. Their faith and their love survived many losses: an infant son, a daughter's eyesight, and countless crops destroyed by hail, pestilence, and drought. Michael Landon played Charles—handsome and manly. Karen Grassle played gentle Caroline, who blushed at his teasing and exclaimed, "Oh, Charles!" His love made her glow, and she would follow him anywhere, through any trial.

That's the kind of bride for which our God longs—not one who will follow Him only for richer, for better, and for health, but one who so loves Him that, as long as she has Him, she will be content in whatever circumstances life may bring, forsaking all others, all the days of her life.

You see, idolatry is about what we love. Do we love God? Or do we use Him to try to get what we *really* love?

In the beginning, Israel did seem to love God. God remembers her fondly at the start of her pilgrimage, when He first rescued her from her slavery in Egypt. In response to the Red Sea closing over her enemies, she took up her tambourine and danced, ready to follow this wonderful God anywhere.

As Derek Kidner writes, "There is a freshness of spring in the Lord's first words to Israel [in Jeremiah 2:2], recapturing the ardour of young love—that readiness of the beloved to go anywhere, put up with anything, so long as it could be shared with her partner, and on his side the fierce protectiveness that would brook no rival, no assault to her honor."[30]

And yes, God did protect her, a knight wielding his sword for the honor of his princess. As we read in Jeremiah:

> Israel was holy to the LORD,
>   the firstfruits of his harvest.
> All who ate of it incurred guilt;
>   disaster came upon them,
>   declares the LORD.
>
> (Jeremiah 2:3)

But the honeymoon is short-lived. The Israelites are still in bondage to the power of sin, to the inward slavery of their idols of security—even the security of slavery. They have not journeyed far when they begin to complain about God's way of rescuing them. They remember with fondness their days in Egypt, weeping and saying, "Oh, that we had meat to eat! We remember the fish we ate in Egypt that cost nothing, the cucumbers, the melons, the leeks, the onions, and the garlic. But now our strength is dried up, and there is nothing at all but this manna to look at" (Numbers 11:4–6).

Their memory is poor. The fish in Egypt were not free at all but came at an enormous cost. Pastor Kevin Cawley says that this would be like a young girl who had been kidnapped and forced to sell her body as a sex slave going on and on about the generosity of her pimp in letting her get all the chips and soda she wanted at the Kwik Trip.

The Israelites' cravings reflect the health of their soul, just as our cravings are a barometer for our soul health. As Cawley says, the Israelites' desire to return to Egypt "had zilch to do with their menu and everything to do with their heart. They are thinking, *If I only had _____ then I'd be happy* . . . Sin is not just junk you do. It is a heart problem. A power, a force that controls us from the inside. This is a deeper slavery than what they experienced in Egypt."[31]

WHAT WRONG DID YOU FIND IN ME?

As Israel questions her rescuer, the Lord wants to know why she is so fickle, forgetting His mercy, forgetting His sacrifice, His miracles, and His love. Again and again in Scripture, God recounts His pain at being forgotten:

They did not remember his power
or the day when he redeemed them from the foe.

(Psalm 78:42)

I wrapped you in fine linen and covered you with silk.
. . . But you trusted in your beauty and played the whore
because of your renown and lavished your whorings on
any passerby.

(Ezekiel 16:10, 15)

Can a virgin forget her ornaments,
or a bride her attire?
Yet my people have forgotten me
days without number.

(Jeremiah 2:32)

How could Israel forget her great rescue from slavery?
How could she forget how God protected her sons with the
Passover Lamb? How could she forget the parting of the Red
Sea? And how can we forget so great a salvation?

The reality is that it isn't so much that we forget (though
we certainly can push God's provision back in our memory)
but that so often we want His "presents" more than His "presence." We love God for what He can give us and not for His
beauty. We want answers to our prayers and we want Him to
protect us from suffering. We want an ideal Christian family
with no disruptions to that picture.

We are no Caroline Ingalls. We have not been ready to
follow our Bridegroom anywhere.

If you love someone for who he is and not for what he can give you, then you are willing to sacrifice. But if you don't love him for him, then sacrifice feels like slavery and you look elsewhere for satisfaction.

I remember when a friend of mine at Northwestern University was going through what was termed "senior panic." She would be graduating soon and there was no engagement ring on her finger. She wanted the security and the status of being a wife. A year before, she had broken off with a young man she did not love, but now she went back to him, telling him she had made a mistake. They became engaged. One night, after talking to him on the phone, she came to my room, flopped on my bed, and said, "Oh, Dee, I hate the sound of his voice." Yet she married him—not for him, but for what he could give her.

God longs for a bride who loves Him for Him and not for what He can give her. He is, as Bernard of Clairvaux put it, "a shy lover."[32] He is aware of those who long for Him and of those who are being untrue—who are, so to speak, in bed with other lovers.

To communicate this, Jeremiah turns to a word picture that is so vivid and so sexual that translators are bashful about translating it literally. But God is making a point that our attraction to our idols is as powerful as sexual attraction. One well-known teacher says the best translation is "spread our legs." Derek Kidner, likewise, says that what some translators translate "bowed down" is better rendered "sprawled out,"[33] as the New English Bible does:

Instead, you gave yourself to other gods
   on every high hill
   and under every green tree,
like a prostitute sprawls out before her lovers.

                                 (Jeremiah 3:6)

Counselors testify that the unfaithfulness of a spouse ranks near the top of the charts for emotional distress. When the one to whom you have given your life and to whom you have made yourself naked and vulnerable betrays you with another, it is akin to having that spouse come after you wielding an ax.

Both idolatry and adultery are powerful word pictures because this language awakens us to the truth that sin is not breaking rules but breaking God's heart. It doesn't seem so terrible to "break a rule." But realizing that our idolatry breaks God's heart is an important step toward returning to the One who saves us.

SNIFFING THE WIND

Jeremiah uses another vivid word picture—of an animal in heat who simply cannot be corralled—to remind us how dangerous our idols can be:

Look at the tracks you've left behind in the valley.
   How do you account for what is written
   in the desert dust—
Tracks of a camel in heat, running this way and that,
   tracks of a wild donkey in rut,
Sniffing the wind for the slightest scent of sex.

Who could possibly corral her!
On the hunt for sex, sex, and more sex—
   insatiable, indiscriminate, promiscuous.

               (Jeremiah 2:23–24, MSG)

When I was seven, our springer spaniel was going through her first heat. My parents, under the advice of the vet, had decided to wait to have her spayed until she was a year old. They did not, however, want her to have puppies. So when they were going out for a few hours, my older sisters and I got stern instructions from Dad: "Keep Chloe *inside*. No matter how badly she wants out, *don't, under any circumstances, let her out.*"

My sisters obeyed, but I only half-obeyed. I felt sorry for her as she whimpered and pawed frantically at the door. I decided to take her to the second-story porch that ran between my bedroom and the garage roof. There was a four-foot railing and a long drop to the ground, so I was sure Chloe would be corralled. But when a male boxer appeared yipping below, Chloe became frantic: circling, crying, and suddenly clawing her way up the shingles on the garage roof. I grabbed her around the middle, trying to hold on to her, but she had developed Herculean strength. She squirmed out of my grasp and leapt from the roof to the driveway. Somehow she survived, mated, and bequeathed to our family a large litter of springer-boxer puppies.

Jeremiah points to animals in heat to show us how strong our cravings are. This is the drive that makes cats howl, salmon batter themselves against the rocks as they swim upstream, and camels leave restless tracks all over the desert.

We have an attraction to sin that is as strong as the animal sexual attraction. Let it in, and it develops a life of its own that is driven, dangerous, and destructive. It may seem harmless at first. We justify "one time" of shading the truth, or masturbating, or flirting with a married man, or watching the beginning of an occult movie. But when we tell ourselves, "Just this once, and I'll do better tomorrow," we have given the enemy a foothold.

We need to fear sin not only because it breaks the heart of God but also because it is addictive. God likens sin to a crouching beast ready to spring. God comes to Cain when he is angry with his brother and tells him if he does what is right, he will be accepted, but if he does not, "sin is crouching at the door. Its desire is for you, but you must rule over it" (Genesis 4:7).

When Cain would not repent of his jealousy, it grew, and he murdered his brother.

When we do not flee temptation but flirt with it, we've opened the door to the beast. Then the beast comes in and we cry out with Paul: "I do not understand my own actions. For I do not do what I want, but I do the very thing I hate" (Romans 7:15).

INTERNAL SLAVERY

Being rescued from external slavery is always easier than being rescued from internal slavery, from the beast within. How clearly this is illustrated by today's holocaust: the sex trade of young girls.

In their Pulitzer Prize-winning book *Half the Sky*, Nicholas Kristof and his wife, Sheryl WuDunn, report on this worldwide slavery, telling stories of girls who had been kidnapped or taken from their families on a ruse and then sold as sex slaves. These girls—many under ten years of age—are drugged, beaten, raped, and forced to sell their bodies night after night. It is another holocaust, and the numbers are beyond imagination.

What Kristof reports is that it is far more effective to crack down on the perpetrators than to try to rescue the victims. That is because rescuing the girls from external slavery is the "easy part," but rescuing them from the beast within, such as the drug addictions that cause them to return or the shame they feel, is enormously challenging. They keep returning to their abusers.

Kristof tells of rescuing Momm, a Cambodian teen who had been enslaved for five years. Momm was on the edge of a breakdown—sobbing one moment, laughing hysterically the next. She seized the chance to escape, promising she'd never return. When Kristof drove Momm back to her village, Momm saw her aunt, screamed, and leapt out of the moving car.

> A moment later, it seemed as if everybody in the village was shrieking and running up to Momm. Momm's mother was at her stall in the market a mile away when a child ran up to tell her that Momm had returned. Her mother started sprinting back to the village, tears streaming down her cheeks. . . . It was ninety minutes before the shouting died away and the eyes dried, and then there was an impromptu feast.[34]

Truly it was a great rescue—and there was singing and dancing and celebrating, reminiscent of the singing and dancing of Miriam and the Israelite women when they were rescued out of their slavery in Egypt.

But as with the Israelites, the celebration didn't last long. Early one morning Momm left her father and her mother without a word and returned to her pimp in Poipet. Like many girls in sex slavery, she had been given methamphetamine to keep her compliant. The craving had overwhelmed her. No doubt she thought, *I just have to have this or I can't go on.* Perhaps she imagined she'd be able to escape after she got it, but even if she didn't, she thought, *I have to have this.*

Sin is addictive.

God has given us a great salvation—but getting out is the easy part. Staying out is harder, for we have sinful cravings in our souls.

In Jeremiah 2, the prophet breaks through the denial of the Israelites. They now admit they are in bondage, but they say, in the language of addicts:

> It is hopeless,
>> for I have loved foreigners,
>> and after them I will go.

(Jeremiah 2:25)

Our idols have a hold over us as strong as the hold of drugs. They make us do what we do not want to do.

When we cannot help ourselves, when we are holed up like prisoners in chains, sometimes the only thing that will set us free is an earthquake.

Again and again women have told me that they did not come to their senses until their worlds were shaken. The author of Hebrews tells us that when God shakes our world, He is removing the things that can be shaken "in order that the things that cannot be shaken may remain" (Hebrews 12:27).

Is it possible that our trials are really our friends?

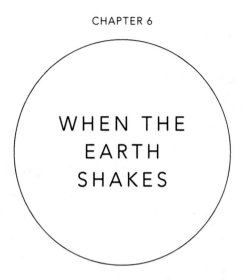

CHAPTER 6

WHEN THE
EARTH
SHAKES

How can I trust a lover who is so wild? . . .
There's only one possible answer: You could
trust him if you knew his heart was good.

—Brent Curtis and John Eldredge, *A Sacred Romance*

From our cabin in Wisconsin there's a long, sweet swim to a raft anchored a few football fields' length out. It belongs to the Reeves, dear generational friends who are like family. Their men do all the work of hauling the raft out and in each summer, of rescuing, repairing, and returning it to the depths when storms on Green Bay overpower it. Those four-foot waves can break the heavy chain to the anchor as if it were a string, carrying the six-hundred-pound raft to shore and tossing it up on the rocks as if it were a child's plastic inner tube. Sometimes we stand inside the safety of our cabins and watch, in awe of the storm, in awe of the power of God.

It's work to keep a raft floating on this capricious bay of Lake Michigan, so I am thankful for what these men do. I'm also thankful that they hospitably urge us to swim to it whenever we like. Swimming in an open bay is a balm to my soul. Plunging into the water, I'm weightless and free, gliding through an underwater world. Calmed by the silence and soothed by the caress of the water slipping over my skin, I've had some of my clearest thoughts during this swim and my best conversations with others. So it was this last Fourth of July weekend. My daughter Sally and I had been reading on the dock, the sun warming our shoulders, when she stood up, stretched, and asked, "Ready to swim to the raft?"

As we side-stroked our way through the flat-calm bay, she asked, "Mom, do you really think, as Ann Voskamp does, that all is grace? That everything, even the really hard things in life, is part of God's grace?" (Sally had recently read and enjoyed Voskamp's book, *One Thousand Gifts*.)

I swim, contemplating my response. Slowly I say, "Yes. I know it doesn't feel like that when things are shaken. Yet looking back, I can see not only that He was with me through the worst things, but that He taught me what is eternal and what is not."

Sally is silent. Her world has been shaken more than the worlds of most thirty-somethings. She plunges under the water and swims. When her blond head emerges, fifteen feet ahead, she flips on her back and floats, looking up at the white clouds and seagulls gliding high in the azure sky. Finally she says, "I can accept that He was with me and that He brings good out of sorrow . . ."

"But . . . ?"

"I don't know. Ann says a good God plans *everything*. She quotes Amos: 'Does disaster come upon a city unless the LORD has planned it?'"

We swim in silence. Hard thoughts. I am remembering a video on suffering based on Tim Keller's book *The Reason for God*. He talked about how a six-year-old may not understand a parent's reasons for depriving him, and he may truly suffer. Then Keller asked the panel of six articulate people who were not Christians, "Is it possible we are all six-year-olds when it comes to understanding the ways of God?"[35]

I say to my daughter, "Honey, I surely would never attempt to explain the Holocaust or your own personal and terrible pain. But I know God is sovereign and nothing slips through His fingers without Him willing it. I know it was God, and not Satan, who *originated* the conversation that would shake Job's world. And at the end of the book of Job, God never gives Job a reason. He simply points to the seas, the stars, and the seasons as evidence that He knows what He is doing. And Job is silenced, broken, and repentant. I think it really may be true that we are six-year-olds when it comes to fathoming God."

She nods, though sorrow is in her eyes. I think of how she screamed when her dad was taking his last breaths, "Daddy, don't leave me!" How she punched a hole in the wall when he did.

"I know He weeps with you, honey. When He shook Mary of Bethany's world, even though He knew He was going to bring her brother back to life, He wept with her. He did have a purpose in allowing Lazarus' death, but that didn't mean He didn't care about the sorrow it caused. Could Keller be right—that we are six-year-olds, at best? Think about how your little Sadie responds when you pull her away from something that could hurt her, like you did last night with the fire."

We both smile, remembering one-year-old Sadie's familiar breakdown pattern, especially if Sally has uttered a sharp, "No, Sadie!" We know a storm is on the horizon when Sadie's bottom lip protrudes and trembles. Next, her astonished blue eyes fill with rain, and finally the tempest bursts, releasing heartbroken sobs, shaking her whole body. She really is suffering. In the midst of her pain, however, she is smarter than many of us, for her chubby arms lift to the very one who caused her pain, the one who is so eager to scoop her up and hold her close, who will sway and whisper, "Hush-a-bye, my little one. Mommy loves you so."

We reach the raft, climbing the ladder and stretching out to be warmed by the sun, contemplating, as well as six-year-olds are able to do, the profundity of God.

THE MYSTERY OF GOD

When my firstborn, J. R., was three, he and I had the respiratory flu. I was trying to watch him and his newborn brother while resting on the sofa. When all was too quiet, I found J. R. sitting cross-legged behind the bathroom door with orange powder around his mouth and an empty bottle of baby aspirin in his lap. In a panic, I called Steve and he told me to give him syrup of ipecac right away to make him vomit. As the ipecac took effect, I held my little boy, rubbing his back as he retched over the toilet. He thought I was punishing him—a cruel and unusual punishment. Between his violent spasms of vomiting, J. R. would gasp for air and plead: "Mommy! I'm sorry! Please stop! I promise I'm sorry!"

I was not bringing judgment but mercy—but at three, he could not see it. Likewise, when God shakes the world of a believer, it is no longer judgment but mercy. We have stones in our hearts, and shaking can loosen those stones so that they may be removed. God's purpose is healing.

If you would ask me to name my ten favorite books of all time, one would be *A Severe Mercy* by Sheldon Vanauken. Just seeing its burgundy spine on my bookshelf releases warmth in my soul. Oh! How drawn I was to the romance of this beautiful couple, looking in their photographs like young Kennedys hopelessly in love. The remarkableness of their love story "lay *not*," as Vanauken put it, "in our falling quite desperately in love—many have experienced that glory—but in what we made of that love."[36] I was mesmerized by their plan of erecting a "shining barrier" to protect the perpetual springtime of their love, to share *everything* so as to create "a thousand strands twisted into something unbreakable." They would guard against "creeping separateness" and sail off alone into the sunset in *The Grey Goose* (their sailboat named after the monogamous waterbird who, if his mate is killed, flies on alone for the rest of his life). They would not, they decided, have children, for children might breach "their shining barrier."

When I read *A Severe Mercy* in my early thirties, though I sensed their blindness in not having children, I didn't recognize the idolatry. It is easier to see idolatry when the idol is overeating, overdrinking, or overspending. But this was marriage. Could there ever be overloving?

Reading the book when I was older and somewhat wiser, I began to see the red flags early on. Van described their goal: "We would become as close as two human beings could become—closer than two people who had ever been born. Whatever storms might come . . . there would be a bedrock closeness."[37]

That's what idols promise. To be a bedrock, a solid rock. But the storm came. The first happened when Davy (her name was Jean Davis, and Van called her Davy) completely surrendered to Christ through their friendship with C. S. Lewis. Though Van was being intellectually persuaded concerning the truths of Christianity, he was holding back. But not Davy. Van said, "For Davy it really was 'overwhelmingly first'—nothing held back. She was literally pouring out her life in Christ's service."[38] Because Van had not yet fully surrendered, it was the first breach into "the shining barrier." It was not that Davy did not still love Van enormously, but that now she loved Christ more, which is how it ought to be. But now, as C. S. Lewis said, Van was jealous of God.

And then, the earthquake. Davy's illness and death, while they were just in their thirties, breaking their bedrock marriage into a thousand pieces, tearing down their shining barrier. Nothing shakes our idols like death. Death shows us, like nothing else, how helpless our idols are. As Jeremiah said:

> But where are your gods
> that you made for yourself?

Let them arise, if they can save you,
In your time of trouble.

(Jeremiah 2:28)

What was the god that Van and Davy had made for themselves? Their marriage. Their love. But, as C. S. Lewis told Van, marriage was not made "to be its Own End." All God's good gifts are given as a blessing, but ultimately, to glorify Him. As Lewis wrote to Van, "One way or another the thing had to die. Perpetual springtime is not allowed. You were not cutting the wood of life according to the grain. There are various possible ways in which it could have died tho' both the parties went on living. You have been treated with a severe mercy."[39]

What did Lewis mean? I believe he meant that when suffering comes, whether caused or permitted by God, it will reveal what is eternal and what is not. Pain has a refining work to do in us if we are open to it, revealing the futility of our idols and the solidness of God. Suffering, indeed, can be "a severe mercy."

At the time of my husband's cancer and death, I would have given a good (and deserved) karate kick to anyone who told me that I would grow from that experience. That I might look back and say this was a grace disguised. Now, though, I see that I have experienced more growth through Steve's death than in any other span of my Christian life.

As Joni Eareckson Tada, who has lived most of her life in a wheelchair, observes, "God's purpose is not to make us healthy, wealthy, or even happy (though it pleases Him to do so), but to make us holy. . . . God cares most—not about making us comfortable—but about teaching us to hate our sins, grow up spiritually, and love Him."[40]

Seeing suffering as "a severe mercy" can open our eyes to our idols like nothing else can.

A SEVERE MERCY

Recently, dear friends of mine began walking through the wilderness. Ed was a pastor with a great deal of warmth who elevated Scripture, but when I visited his church and listened to him preach, his sermon seemed man-centered instead of gospel-centered. Man-centered sermons tend to focus on what we can do instead of on the glory and the power of God. Though this may not be the pastor's intention, the effect is that individuals listening then try to change themselves mechanically instead of concentrating on intimacy with God. And basically—it doesn't work. Unless Christ is continually exalted, our hearts remain cold, and we do not long to abide in Him, so we do not bear lasting fruit.

I thought about telling Ed about a wonderful series on gospel-centered preaching I had listened to. But since most pastors do not welcome unsolicited suggestions on how to be a better preacher, I held back. However, when the church gave Ed a sabbatical, I emailed him, telling him my own speaking had improved dramatically since listening to seventeen messages from Ed Clowney and Tim Keller on how to preach to the heart. I gave him the iTunes link in case he was interested in listening during his sabbatical.[41]

He was. He listened to every message and took dozens of pages of notes. He went through a time of personal revival. He was convicted that his preaching was not truly gospel-centered. He returned to the church after the sabbatical, excited, telling the elders that he wanted to lead the church in gospel-centered preaching through Romans. But to my great surprise, the elders did not agree with that direction, and Ed felt, before God, that he had to resign. He preached three more Sundays (and I visited and was brought to tears by the power of his preaching) and then he was without a job. His wife, Cynthia, who had thrown herself into being a pastor's wife, was stripped of all those ministries. She assumed her husband would find another pastorate by the next year, so she also did not sign her teaching contract with a Christian classical school for the next year.

But it has been a year and no door has opened. Ed is driving a bus to put food on the table. Cynthia is tutoring where she can. They have sold their home and are temporarily living with friends. As Cynthia puts it, "We are homeless!"

How have they responded? They each say this time has been "a severe mercy," for it is revealing hidden idols of their heart. I sat and listened to them each confess, telling me how this time of loss has been a good thing. Together they took a discipleship class with World Harvest Mission called Sonship, continuing to grow in their understanding of gospel-centered theology. They are endeavoring to "wait well" for a door to open welcoming Ed to preach in the way he now longs to preach.

Cynthia and I took a prayer walk together along the icy Missouri River. It was so cold we could see our breath as the words tumbled out of our mouths, our hearts fervent about being delivered from idolatry.

Cynthia said, "You know how in Jeremiah 2 God says we are adulteresses—that we have spread our legs for other lovers?"

"Oh my, yes."

As Cynthia spoke, I was wondering where she could be going, for to me, she was a woman passionate for God. She was an energetic and creative teacher—the students almost unanimously say she was the best teacher they had at that school. Likewise, when Cynthia was behind a retreat, a ministry, or a Sunday school class, it was always amazing.

"So, Cynthia, what was your idol?"

"Achievement. My idol, my false lover, was—*is*—achievement! I always felt I was special and that others were blessed to know me. I thought, *I'm a competent person and they would want a competent person to do this.*"

She paused, tears coming to her eyes. "I was worshiping myself and my achievement. It was my identity, it was works righteousness, it was my lover. Having my status taken from me has been a good thing. God is breaking up my heart idol. It *is* a severe mercy."

As I listened to her, I thought, *This is how someone who trusts Christ responds to suffering. She presses in. She asks for His light to shine into her darkness.*

When we back away from God in the midst of suffering, we are not only blanketing His light, we are also cutting off our only lifeline. He is the One, and the only One, who can help us when real trouble comes. And He will. After all, He is the great I AM.

THE GREAT I AM

When the waters roar and the mountains tremble for Martha of Bethany, her idol of control shatters. Despite her competence, she cannot stop her brother from dying. When Jesus finally comes, she is the first out to meet Him, accusing, "Lord, if you had been here, my brother would not have died" (John 11:21).

Jesus doesn't explain Himself. Instead, He makes a stunning revelation to her: "I am the resurrection and the life. Whoever believes in me, though he die, yet shall he live, and everyone who lives and believes in me shall never die. Do you believe this?" (John 11:25–26).

We cannot fully appreciate the words of Jesus unless we understand that He, in saying "*I am* the resurrection," is claiming deity. Eight times in John's Gospel, including here, Jesus refers to Himself as the great "I AM." This, according to the Septuagint, (the Greek translation of the Hebrew scriptures in Jesus' day), is the exact same phrase, the double I am, that God gave to Moses when Moses asked God to tell him His name. God said, "I AM WHO I AM. . . . Say this to the people of Israel, 'I AM has sent me to you'" (Exodus 3:14).

Therefore, every time Jesus says one of the great I AMs in John's Gospel, He is claiming to be God. Each time He identifies Himself as the great I AM, His friends are in awe and His enemies want to kill him. They recognize He is making a claim to deity. As R. C. Sproul puts it:

This is one of the purest and unvarnished declarations of Deity that Jesus ever makes during His ministry, and it was not missed by His audience as they took up stones to throw at Him. They heard in His claim a claim to Deity.

He comes as the Resurrection.

He comes as the Bread of Life.

He comes as the Door.

He comes as the Light.

He comes as the Way, and the Truth, and the Life.

He comes as the Good Shepherd.

He comes as the Vine.

He is the One who could say, Before Abraham was, I AM.[42]

Do you see? When the mountains fall into the sea, when our idols crumble, we still have the great I AM. This is what Jesus is telling Martha. He can be trusted—and nothing is beyond His control, not even death. Martha can let Him take over.

She responds in faith: "Yes, Lord; I believe that you are the Christ, the Son of God, who is coming into the world" (John 11:27).

Like my granddaughter Sadie, Martha is lifting her arms to the one who allowed her pain. For she sees who He is. She surrenders to the great I AM.

Martha then runs to get her sister, Mary. (Do you see the change? Before, she was trying to get Mary away from Jesus and into the kitchen. Now she's telling Mary to go to Jesus.) Mary runs to Jesus, falls at His feet, and says the same thing her sister said: "Lord, if you had been here, my brother would not have died" (John 11:32). But though she says the same thing, she must have a different attitude, for Jesus does not confront her. He is so overcome with sorrow that He cannot speak. All He does is weep.

This speaks profoundly to me, and I hope to you. Jesus cares about our suffering. He permits suffering for mysterious reasons, but that doesn't mean He doesn't weep. He knows He is about to stop this funeral, but He looks down through the ages and knows there are many funerals He will not stop. He weeps. He is angry, as well, at the prince of this world.

Yet Jesus *is* greater than Satan, for Jesus takes what Satan is trying to accomplish and turns it on its head. Satan wants Martha and Mary to back up from Jesus, but instead they draw nearer to Him. Satan wants to defame God's name with the death of Lazarus, but instead, when Jesus brings Lazarus back from the dead, God is glorified.

Satan loves it when we cling to our idols instead of to God, but when Satan is allowed to shake our world, it reveals the impotence of our idols. Not only that, but suffering can cause us to have an intimate experience with Jesus that we might not otherwise have had. As one of my friends said, "Dee, the fact that suffering leads to intimacy is stunning to me."

Yes.

WHEN THE EARTH SHOOK

We are six-year-olds when it comes to understanding the mystery of suffering. We cannot know the reason God allows it, but we *can* know what the reason is not.

When Jesus hung on the cross for us, giving up His last breath, "the earth shook, and the rocks were split" (Matthew

27:51). Truly God's judgment shook the world. So when you suffer now as a believer, *it is not because God is angry with you, because Jesus took God's anger that day on the cross.*

Jesus cried, "It is finished," so may we let it be! Let us trust that He is not punishing us, for that is finished. When we do feel pain, whatever the reason, He feels it as well. He has allowed it for a purpose we often can't fully understand—so He weeps with us. He also whispers to us, "Hush-a-bye, your Abba loves you."

Lift your arms to Him, and let the One who allowed this pain be your comfort, be your God. He has a power to help us—a power we cannot find in ourselves.

Every other religion tells its followers that they have a power in themselves. They tell them they can rescue themselves by walking through the pillars, climbing the steps, obeying the rules. Only Christianity gives us a power outside of ourselves. God knows we cannot rescue ourselves, so He comes running.

That's where we are going next in Part 3—to understanding *how* to let Him rescue you.

PART 3

Power from on High

He reached down from on high

and took hold of me;

he drew me out of deep waters.

————

Psalm 18:16, NIV

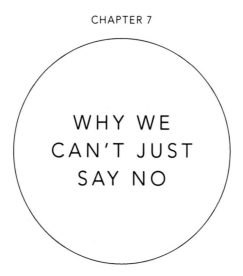

CHAPTER 7

WHY WE
CAN'T JUST
SAY NO

*I do not do what I want to do, but I do the very thing I
hate. . . . Who will deliver me from this body of death?
Thanks be to God through Jesus Christ our Lord!*

—Romans 7:15, 24–25

I received a small, blue Schwinn bike for my sixth birthday.
Dad taught me to ride—first with training wheels and then by
running beside me, laughing along with his euphoric daughter.
I pedaled proudly all the way down the block and back, a bit
wobbly, but staying erect.

Two weeks later my parents were departing for a long-
anticipated two-week vacation to Acapulco, Mexico. As they
left my older sisters and me in the care of white-haired Mrs.
Hahn, my dad turned and cupped my face in his hands. "Be
careful on your new bike, Deedle." I nodded solemnly. Then,

as an afterthought, he said, "Don't take your bike up to Ridge Hill." Immediately I thought, *Why, I would absolutely fly going down that hill!*

I was distracted in my first-grade class the next day, for I kept thinking of how exciting it would be to fly down Ridge Hill, the street behind our house. As soon as I got home, I told Mrs. Hahn I was going out to ride my new bike, and I walked my bike to the top of Ridge Hill. I had a moment of fear surveying the steep incline, and a brief warning flash of my father's commandment, but still, I didn't want to miss the thrill. So I jumped on, barreled down, didn't make the turn, and plowed into a tree in the Rolfs' yard. I vaguely remember adults yelling, sirens wailing, someone lifting me onto something hard, and finally awaking in enormous pain in a hospital bed.

My parents were called, and though they had just unpacked in Mexico, they re-packed, left their hotel on the beach, and returned on the next plane back. (There were only propeller planes for the public then—and it was a long trip from Acapulco to West Bend, Wisconsin.) I was afraid Dad would be fiercely angry, but I was such a sorry sight that he simply cradled me and wept.

The law can inspire us to do wrong, but the law itself is not wrong. Dad was right when he told me to be careful on my bike and forbade me from riding down Ridge Hill. And the commandments of our heavenly Father are true and righteous altogether. Each one will protect us, guide us, and lead us into a flourishing life. When God sees us ignore them, He is brokenhearted not only because we have ignored Him but also because He sees us plow into trees and destroy ourselves. The law is meant to protect.

So if that law is not wrong, what *is* wrong?

A hidden force within us cannot be conquered by our own willpower. It is that epi-desire that is as overpowering as the animal sex drive. We cannot overcome it on our own.

Often the approach in both the world and in the church is to scold ourselves, using the approach of the "law." I've done it. I've slapped my own hand when I've reached for the chips, saying, "Bad Dee Dee." Abusive people who hurt others often feel terrible afterward, hating themselves and promising, with weeping, to never hit the person they love again. Advertisements tell teens to "just say no" to drugs. Sexual abstinence programs take the same approach.

We must understand why this approach lacks power and can actually boomerang, inciting us to do evil.

I have gone to a Weight Watchers meeting *determined* to turn over a new leaf, copied down the recipe for Weight Watchers brownies, whipped them up, and then, instead of having just one, devoured half the pan. Then I'd despair and wonder if I could ever be free.

In the same way, the early Christian leader Augustine despaired of being set free of his sexual promiscuity. He wrote, "The enemy had a grip on my will and so made a chain to hold me prisoner."[43]

Rebellion grows deep in our souls, becoming darker and darker, turning Dr. Jekyll into Mr. Hyde. We are, in fact, more depraved than we ever want to think, and the roots of our sin are strong and slippery. When the law is used by itself through a sermon, a sexual abstinence class, or our own self-talk, it's like trying to grip those roots with plastic children's scissors. It slips away repeatedly until we lament, like the Israelites in Jeremiah 2, "It is hopeless!" (verse 25). Paul cried, "Wretched man that I am! Who will deliver me from this body of death?" But here, in the New Testament, we have the answer, the mystery, for Paul also says, "Thanks be to God through Jesus Christ our Lord!" (Romans 7:24–25).

THE LAW BY ITSELF LACKS TEETH

The approach of "just say no" to drugs, to alcohol, and to sex outside of marriage is not completely devoid of value. By making people aware of the painful consequences of unwise choices, this approach enables some to exercise restraint.

In a sexual abstinence program, students are told that sex outside of marriage results in disease, broken hearts, and unwanted pregnancies. A diet program will tell dieters that poor eating habits will result in a lack of energy, a lack of health, and a lack of enjoyment in life. A college ethics class will tell business students that lying and cheating to get money may land them in jail or may hurt their reputation and result in a loss of return clients. The problem is, because we cherish our idols, we are more apt to devise schemes to circumvent negative consequences than to turn from the idols themselves.

Young people think they can get around the negative consequences of sex outside of marriage by using condoms. They also deceive themselves into thinking that this teenage love is forever. When a young Johnny Depp had "Winona Forever" tattooed on his arm, he meant it. But it wasn't forever. So, with sad resignation, he removed two letters and made what he was quite sure would always be true: "Wino Forever."

Many dieters discovered they could circumvent diets of deprivation and still lose weight by going on a low- or no-carb diet. They could still enjoy steak and mushrooms, strawberries and whipped cream, and crab legs dripping in butter—and lose weight! The problem is, our bodies need carbohydrates, and all that fat leads to heart attacks—and as soon as you reintroduce carbs into the diet, the lost weight plus more comes back on. Many give up and resign themselves to being overweight.

When the only incentive to being honest in business is to avoid painful consequences, people are apt to devise ways to hide their lying or their cheating.

In other words, we try to circumvent the consequences of breaking the law, so the law lacks teeth. But there is an even deeper problem with the law.

The "law," or the rule we recite to ourselves, can actually boomerang and increase our tendency toward lustful behaviors. Children may go home from sex education classes with premature sexual awakenings. Likewise, banned books skyrocket to the top of the bestseller list. My friend Kim remembers her parents giving her and her siblings a list of television shows they should not watch—and of course, those were the shows they looked up and watched when their parents left to go out for an evening. Eugene Peterson translates Romans 7:8 like this in *The Message*: "The law code started out as an excellent piece of work. What happened, though, was that sin found a way to pervert the command into a temptation, making a piece of 'forbidden fruit' out of it. The law code, instead of being used to guide me, was used to seduce me."

Nowhere is this more clearly illustrated than in the hearts of those behind prison walls.

BEHIND PRISON WALLS

I have been involved in prison ministry for many years, but my commitment to it accelerated dramatically in the last five years due to two events in my life. First, I have a nephew who made a foolish and sinful choice and was incarcerated in Texas for four years. He repented deeply, a full U-turn, even before his four years of incarceration started. But his incarceration gave me a firsthand look into the prisons of Texas. Though there are pockets of humanity, I have been shocked at the inhumane treatment, not only in the prisons he was in, but also in other Texas prisons I have visited.

At this writing, there is no air conditioning in Texas prisons, so there are many months when the temperatures can climb to 120 degrees within those metal buildings. A body count is needed each night because some inmates die from the heat. In one prison my nephew was in, the only food was soggy peanut butter sandwiches (prepared a week in advance) and very limited quantities of water. Racism is rampant. Lockdowns are common, where inmates are confined to their cots for weeks or even months. When I visited some women's prisons near Gatesville, I was shown cages that look like dog kennels, where women who are either in danger or considered to be dangerous are kept in solitary confinement. They cannot even stand up.

Some die in those cages. I am aghast and think, *How can this be happening in America?* But it is.

Sometimes when I tell others about this, I get a response such as "Dee, we don't want prison to be like a country club" or "Maybe this will help *those people* think before they commit another criminal act." Anger bubbles up in me, and yet I know they have not seen what I have seen or met the broken women who had their childhoods stolen from them or looked into the prisoners' hopeless eyes. Many were raped repeatedly as girls, were given hard drugs, and were mentored in the ways of darkness. These women *have* tried to change but cannot pull themselves out of the quicksand. I know people think we can "just say no" to destructive behavior. I know that is the erroneous thinking behind the inhumanity of "Texas tough." Elected officials who resist prison reform seem to think, *If we make criminals miserable enough in prison, then they will "just say no" to drugs, to prostitution, to returning to dysfunctional families or boyfriends.*

But it isn't working. Eighty-five percent of those who are in Texas prisons return. It isn't that they *want* to return to prison; it is that there is a dark power within each person that cannot be overcome by willpower alone. Each of us has an enemy working against us by breathing lies to us. Charles Colson, founder of Prison Fellowship, aptly observed that the only two ways inmates avoid returning to prison are to die or to find Christ.

In God's sovereignty, God also increased my participation in prison ministry by crossing my path with Linda Strom's path. God is using Linda mightily to help inmates find Christ. Have you ever had the experience of meeting someone and sensing such a rapport that you simply knew in your deepest being that God had ordained your friendship? That's how it was for Linda and me. We laugh at the unusual way God crossed our paths, for we each uncharacteristically agreed to take part in a "telephone Bible study" for authors and speakers. Because it wasn't video, we had to identify ourselves each time we made a comment, and because there were several women who shared the same first name, we would hear, "This is Linda from Nashville," or "Linda from Ontario," or "Linda from Texas." We were confused most of the time! Linda (from Texas) and I each privately thought, *Why did I commit to this?*

But as the weeks passed, I began to perk up each time "Linda from Texas" spoke. Invisible threads connected us—a love for the Word, an interest in prison ministry, beloved husbands who had died of cancer in their prime, roots in Door County, Wisconsin. And there was something else—a sacred sense that God might be drawing us together.

Finally we met in person. I was in awe of Linda's abandonment to Christ. The first time she visited the prisons in Texas, she said to her late husband, Dallas, "Let's sell our home in Wisconsin, move down here, and give the rest of our lives to prison ministry." Dallas patted her knee and told her to slow down. Yet God persuaded him that that was exactly what He was calling him and Linda to do. What strikes me whenever I am with Linda is her enormous joy—despite losing her husband, despite facing enormous challenges in her ministry, she often will say to me, "I'm so happy." Why? It's Jesus welling up in her. There is never a death to self without a corresponding resurrection from Him. He is intimate with her, the Lover of her Soul, and when you meet her, you cannot help but think, *This is a woman in love.*

One of the evidences that idols are being dismantled in a person can be seen when she cares about the things Jesus cares about—the poor, the downtrodden, the immigrant, the prisoner. She longs, as Mother Teresa did, to minister to the least of these, for she knows that in so doing she is ministering to Jesus. I watch Linda moving from cell to cell, sitting cross-legged on the cement floor, talking to inmate after inmate, her face filled with the love of Christ. Indeed, she is Jesus to these broken souls.

Linda's compassion for the women "behind the fences" comes, in part, from knowing what it is to have your childhood stolen from you. Linda's father was an abusive alcoholic. As a little girl, she and her mother would watch from the window to see how much her dad staggered as he walked from his car to the front door. If he staggered a lot, they would flee and hide in the woods behind their house until they were sure he was asleep and it was safe to go in.

When Linda tells her story in prison, the women listen, and then they confide in her. One such woman was Karla Faye Tucker, whose family started her on cocaine when she was eleven. As a young woman, when out of her mind on drugs, she brutally murdered two people with a pickaxe. Karla was the first woman to be executed in Texas in over one hundred years.

Linda became Karla's mentor for the fourteen years Karla was on death row, then went on to write her biography and carry out Karla's dream of establishing "faith dorms" within the prisons in order to help inmates who come to Christ become disciples. These faith dorms are succeeding—in contrast to the 85 percent recidivism (rate of return of inmates) in the Texas prisons at large, the recidivism rate in the faith dorms is 12 percent. Christ has the power needed to lift one trapped in the spiral of sin.

It wasn't long after Linda and I met when she told me her dream: "Dee, we so need a video Bible study tailored especially for women in prison. Something that would speak directly to them—to their hurts, to their needs. Would you write it? Would you teach it, and we'd film you? We could intersperse it with video clips from Karla—we have so much material from her interviews on *Larry King Live, 20/20, The 700 Club*. Then we could have this material available for prisons everywhere. I'd use it in the faith dorms in Texas. I'd take it to Africa."

That Bible study became a reality.[44] God is bringing it into prisons throughout the United States and Africa, and I am humbled by the response.

The best part of this curriculum is not my teaching but the clips from Karla. They bring tears to my eyes every time I watch them—to see a woman who was so dark, and so in bondage, transformed into a woman with the radiance of an angel puts you in awe of the power of God.

In her testimony, which you can see on my website, Karla tells her story. When a Christian team came into her prison to do a chapel service, Karla went mockingly, but God got a hold of her heart. She stole one of their Bibles because she didn't know they were giving them away. She took it back to her cell and was crouched in the corner reading it when the living Word came and quickened her. Karla didn't remember what part of the Bible she turned to, but suddenly she found herself kneeling on the cell's cement floor, crying, asking God to come into her heart and forgive her.

Read Karla's words, some of which I have italicized, and see, again and again, that this transformation was not from her but a power from on high.

> I don't even know that I felt forgiven at that point, but I know that I felt loved. *It was like God just completely wrapped me up in a cocoon of love. . . . At that point the whole weight of what I had done fell on me.* I realized for the first time that I had brutally murdered two people and that there were people hurting out there because of me—and yet God was saying, "I love you." That I could be so loved unconditionally after I had done something so horrible—*I don't know how to explain it—it's supernatural . . . but He reached down inside of me and ripped up by the very roots the violence in me and poured His love into me.*

Karla went on to tell the truth in court about what she had done, for God was so real to her. She impacted thousands while she was alive, and now her life—through Linda's biography and through the video clips we have of her—is impacting countless thousands.

But it isn't just Karla and the women in prison who need a hand to reach down inside them and rip up by the roots the idols that are keeping them enslaved. We all do. We all need

Someone bigger than ourselves to rescue us. We can't just say no—our idols are too alluring. We need to be drawn to something better. To Someone better.

We need to fall in love.

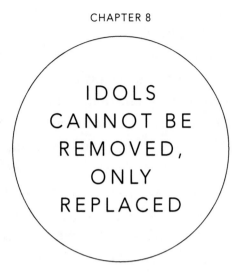

CHAPTER 8

IDOLS
CANNOT BE
REMOVED,
ONLY
REPLACED

*The only way to dispossess the heart of an old affection
is by the expulsive power of a new affection.*

—Thomas Chalmers, "The Expulsive Power of a New Affection"

I met Jack between my junior and senior years of high school, when I spent the summer at Northwestern University. NU had a "cherub program" designed to acquaint potential NU students with the excellencies of Northwestern's speech, debate, and film departments. I became acquainted with the excellencies of Jack Tate, another high schooler spending the summer at the university.

Protected by my parents and my conservative Midwestern values, I was a babe in the woods, vulnerable to Jack's southern charms. He knew much more about winning girls than did the farm boys from West Bend, Wisconsin. He winked, he wooed, and he warmed my heart with flattering phrases. When he asked me to study with him one night, I wasn't sure if he just wanted a study partner or something more. But after studying, as we walked out of the library and into the summer night, fragrant with lilacs, he took my hand to walk me back to Willard Hall. On the way, he led me off the path and into an ivy-covered corner where two sorority houses met. He kissed me passionately, like I'd never been kissed. My head was spinning. My desires had been awakened. This "cherub" had gotten her wings. I could only think about Jack. Life was suddenly electric and my focus was Jack, Jack, Jack. I was infatuated.

Jack and I returned to Northwestern as freshmen. We resumed seeing one another, but now I saw red flags. He flirted with many beautiful Northwestern coeds, pressured me sexually, lost his temper, and had violent mood swings—tender one moment, furious the next.

At times Jack frightened me, and the deepest part of me thought I would be wise to stop seeing him. And yet I couldn't bring myself to completely do that. It wasn't so much that I was afraid of his reaction (though I was), but I feared the emptiness in my life, the vacuum that would be created by his absence. I could not turn away from Jack. I couldn't just say no. As I look back, I realize I was the female counterpart of the youth "without discernment" in Proverbs 7, who was walking toward a dangerous woman, "not knowing it will cost him his life."

But God in His great mercy intervened, diverting me from that destructive path. I think it is very possible that the Lord caused me to notice Steve Brestin. Steve was one of a thousand in a lecture class called Human Behavior. Northwestern University was challenging, and students took copious notes, but Steve simply listened (I learned later that he memorized as the professor spoke). Though Steve was very masculine, he was gentle, others-centered, and kind to everyone. I was intrigued and started sitting directly in front of him, with the far-fetched hope that he might notice me. I started dressing carefully for Human Behavior, donning my pink angora sweater and spraying Lily of the Valley behind my ears. Yet all the while I pretended not to notice him. (It's the dance of wooing—you move back in hope that the man will move forward.)

On a Monday, February 5, Steve leaned forward and, in a deep, masculine voice I came to treasure, said, "I've run out of paper. Would you happen to have any extra paper?" I knew he didn't take notes and didn't use paper, so my hopes soared. Though my heart was beating wildly, I tried to seem nonchalant as I tore pages from my spiral notebook and handed them to him. After class I grabbed my books and hurried out, hoping he would follow.

He did. He caught up with me in front of Deering Library, stepping in front of me and introducing himself. "Hi, I'm Steve Brestin. I've been wanting to meet you." To my embarrassment, I began to tremble visibly. He seemed concerned and asked, "Are you cold?"

"Yes," I lied, "that lake wind . . . "

Steve took off his raincoat and put it around my shoulders. I felt taken care of, cherished. When he asked me if I would go out with him that coming Wednesday night, I threw nonchalance to the wind and said, "I'd love to!"

One date was all it took for both of us. Steve engaged me in conversation like no one had ever done before. He asked me question after question and really listened. He treated people, including me, with such gentle kindness. I kept thinking, *This is a man, not a boy.* When I came home, I remember flopping backward on my bed and exclaiming to my roommate, Heather: "This is the man I am going to marry."

"What about Jack?" she asked.

I shook my head. My heart had been captured by a new affection.

Jack called me that week and invited me to fly down to his home in South Carolina for a long weekend to meet his family. I still remember where I was standing at that crossroads moment. I was next to my bed, looking out the window at the snow-covered campus, nervously fingering the curly telephone cord. If I said no, Jack could get angry enough to drop me. If I said yes, it could endanger my relationship with Steve. Whichever way I went, it could end the relationship with the other.

I said a firm no. I now had the power to say no. Why? It was the expulsive power of a new affection.

I don't know what kind of a man Jack eventually became, but this much I do know: when we were dating, he looked great but was destructive to me. Yet I kept swimming toward him, like a fish swims toward a lure. Even when I began to see the danger, it was hard for me to swim away. What enabled me to finally turn was meeting Steve. I was in love, and I didn't want anything to jeopardize that relationship.

I can also remember a few times when, during our courtship, and even after we were married, an attractive man would flirt with me. The thought I always had, even before I was a Christian, was, *No! I would never do this to Steve!*

In the same way, as we fall deeply in love with Jesus, as that relationship becomes increasingly real and precious to us, we don't want to grieve Him through worshiping other gods; we don't want to push Him away. Remember Joseph's reaction when Potiphar's wife tried to seduce him? He said, "How can I do this great wickedness and sin against God?" (Genesis 39:9). As His love rises in our hearts, it expels what we could not expel by our own willpower. We don't want to do anything to grieve Him or cause us to lose the sense of His sweet presence.

THE EXPULSIVE POWER OF A NEW AFFECTION

Centuries ago, Scottish mathematician and theologian Thomas Chalmers (1780–1847) delivered his now classic sermon "The Expulsive Desire of a New Affection." Chalmers explains that we were made to worship, and our souls will not tolerate a vacuum. He says "a sensitive being" suffers without an object of pursuit, without something to interest his mind and emotions. We will worship, for we cannot help it. The only way to be delivered from a desire is to replace it with a new desire. Chalmers writes, "The most effectual way of withdrawing the mind from one object is not by turning it away . . . but by presenting to its regards another object still more alluring."

Chalmers gives the illustration of a young man who is obsessed with the pleasures of drinking and carousing with women. What could deliver him from that desire? Only an object still more alluring. He might leave the life of pleasure behind by becoming allured by success and material things. His energies would now be redirected toward succeeding in school and obtaining a well-paying job. Again, his mind is put into "busy exercise," and all his energies and thoughts are intent upon the new goal. When this goal is achieved, he will become dissatisfied again, for earthly things—idols—are never able to satisfy what Pascal called our "God-shaped hole."

Chalmers's illustration sounds like the author of Ecclesiastes, who ran headlong into various pursuits, always hoping for fulfillment. He threw himself into worldly wisdom, throwing parties, building palaces and gardens, and acquiring concubines. As long as he was in pursuit, he was excited and energetic. He found some pleasure in each pursuit, as we temporarily do in our idols, but each time he attained his pursuit, he was disillusioned, crying: "All was vanity and a striving after wind, and there was nothing to be gained under the sun" (Ecclesiastes 2:11).

The One who will satisfy is the Lover of our Soul. He is the only One who can replace our idols and bring lasting joy. But *how* does this happen?

We have to fall in love with the Lord. That's the only way His power will rise in us and release us from the grasp of our idols.

That's what released Leah from the idol that was destroying her.

MAYBE MY HUSBAND
WILL LOVE ME NOW

In *The Jesus Storybook Bible*, Sally Lloyd-Jones calls Leah "the girl nobody wanted." Poor Leah has some kind of an eye defect, perhaps cross-eyes or a lazy eye that kept wandering, distracting from whatever beauty she had. Her father, Laban, sees his firstborn daughter as a liability and uses a ruse to "marry her off." During the wedding, in which Jacob thinks he is marrying her gorgeous younger sister, Rachel, Leah's face is heavily veiled—a veil that remains until she is safely in the dark wedding tent. All night long Jacob probably whispers, *Rachel . . . oh, Rachel.* When the sun rises and Jacob looks into Leah's not so lovely eyes, he storms out of their tent and confronts Laban: "What is this you have done to me? Did I not serve you for Rachel?" (Genesis 29:25).

My heart goes out to Leah.

She vulnerably gave her virginity to Jacob—and he despises her.

The shame.

The embarrassment.

There is something worse than being hated, and that is not being thought about at all. Jacob doesn't even think about how his anger would pierce Leah's heart.

When we are ignored, it makes us feel like we aren't real, like we don't matter, like we don't even exist. In *The Book of God*, Walter Wangerin imagines Leah's thoughts concerning Jacob: "He did not look at me with anything at all, neither a thought nor a word nor a feeling. When he looked at me he did not see Leah. He saw not-Rachel."[45]

And so what is normally a good desire, to want a husband's love, grew to an epi-desire in Leah. It isn't hard to imagine her thought life:

If only Jacob would love me, I could be happy.

If only Jacob would love me, I would matter.

If only Jacob would look at me like he looks at Rachel . . .

When the Lord, out of compassion for Leah's loveless marriage, opens her womb, Leah thinks, *If I have a son, then Jacob will love me.*

And Leah has a son—in fact, Leah has many sons. Each time she bears Jacob a son, she gives him a name that revealed her true desires.

Her first son is named Reuben. She says, "For the LORD has looked upon my affliction; for now my husband will love me" (Genesis 29:32). Reuben means "See, a son."

But Jacob does not love Leah. When she gives birth to a second son, she names him Simeon and says, "Because the LORD has heard that I am hated, he has given me this son also" (verse 33). Simeon sounds like the Hebrew word for "heard."

Still, Jacob does not love her. When she bears a third son, she names him Levi, saying, "Now this time my husband will be attached to me, because I have borne him three sons" (verse 34). Levi sounds like the Hebrew rod for "attached."

Still, Jacob does not love her. At that point, Leah can either give up—or turn to the One who will love her.

WHAT, IF YOU LOST IT, WOULD MAKE LIFE NOT WORTH LIVING?

Recently at a speaking engagement, I said, "One of the ways you can identify your idol is by asking yourself, *What, if I lost it, would make life not worth living?*" A woman stood up abruptly, and though she was in the middle of a long row, she was in a panic to get out. She pushed rapidly past women who were scrambling to tuck in their knees and move their purses. I wondered, *Is she sick?* But when she ran up the aisle and out of the sanctuary sobbing, I knew. My question had pierced her heart.

After I finished speaking, her friends pleaded with me to talk to her. "She's a train wreck. She only wants one thing—her husband to come back—and that's not going to happen. Please talk to her."

I tried. Between sobs she told me her story. Her husband had been telling her for years that she was smothering him. "I know I didn't give him any room to breathe. *But I would if he would just come back.*"

I wasn't so sure.

"Have you gotten any counseling?"

"No. No. I don't want that."

"And he separated from you?"

"Yes."

"Did he divorce you?"

She sobbed, nodding. I put my arm around her.

"How long?"

"Two years."

I told her it was all right to grieve.

She pulled away.

"Don't tell me that! I won't grieve. *I only want you to pray that my husband will come back!*"

I told her she needed to let Jesus be her Solid Rock.

"Would that help me get my husband back?"

"Oh, you can't do it that way. You have to really allow Jesus to be your Solid Rock, not just pretend so you might get him back. If Jesus is going to be your Solid Rock, then you need to release your husband."

"*No!*"

I couldn't help her. She was hanging on to a little branch protruding from a cliff. It would not hold her, but I could not convince her to take my hand and get up on the rock. I felt like I was talking to a meth addict—matted hair, wild eyes, shaking hands, and a mind that focused only on what she thought she *had* to have. In the state she was in, even if her husband came back, I knew she would drive him out again, because she wanted him to be what no person can be.

There was a time in our culture when marriage was not seen as a way to meet deep soul needs. Marriage provided support and stability. If you were blessed, there was love as well. But for soul needs, people looked to God and eternity. Today many people, Christians and non-Christians alike, look for a "soul mate" to meet their deepest needs and then they are profoundly disappointed when their spouse cannot meet those needs. I was blessed with an incredible man—but I am so thankful I had a wake-up call early in our marriage that even Steve could not meet my soul needs.[46] I grieved terribly when he died, and still do, but I didn't jump off a bridge, because as wonderful as Steve was, he was not my Savior.

If we don't ever wake up to the reality that our epi-desires will destroy us, we will continue to pursue them relentlessly. And if we do not release our idols, our "Shy Lover" will not come to us. He will not abide another lover.

Leah finally comes to the realization that she must stop desperately pursuing Jacob's love. I can almost see her sitting by the fire, grieving the loss, but letting her dream go up with the smoke, singing the song Bonnie Raitt made famous: "I Can't Make You Love Me (If You Don't)."

Something finally clicks in her heart. I think it is God in His mercy opening Leah's eyes to reality—not just the reality that her marriage could never satisfy her soul needs, but also to the reality that *He* could.

OUR IDOLS ARE NOT OUR FRIENDS

Our idols are like that smiley yellow Pac-Man, except that in this case they look like friends, but—*gulp, gulp, gulp*—they swim through our lives swallowing up our peace, our hope, and our joy.

Leah comes to the realization that Jacob might never love her and that setting her hopes on him was destroying her. She grieves, but she moves on, turning to the only One who can help her.

When Leah has her fourth son, she makes a turn. She doesn't give him a name that sounds like "Maybe my husband will love me now." She names him Judah, which sounds like the Hebrew word for praise. She says, "This time I will praise the LORD" (Genesis 29:35). She turns from her idol and to the Lord.

The Lord is pleased. As she opens her heart to Him, He opens His arms to her. His love is like the sap that rises in the spring, pushing off the dead leaves that have clung to the branches all through the winter. We cannot get rid of those leaves by ourselves, but the expulsive power of God's love can push them off. Leah is changed. *She* is the calm and contented sister now.

I also think Jacob's heart begins to turn toward her. How could he not miss the sharp contrast between Rachel's continued bitterness, a crushed spirit that Proverbs says "dries up the bones" (Proverbs 17:22), and Leah's new contentment, that gentle and quiet spirit that comes from putting your hope in God (1 Peter 3:4–5)?

Before Jacob dies, he asks to be buried in the cave where he buried Leah. In fact, the last words on his dying lips are "and there I buried Leah" (Genesis 49:31). Yet Leah's greatest blessings would only be seen by her in eternity. From her son Levi the whole priesthood descended. She is named in the book of Ruth for "building up the house of Israel." And it is her son Judah, the one whose name means "praise," from whom Jesus Christ, our Messiah, descended! Rachel had what this world values and Leah did not. But as so often happens, it was the great eternal reversal.

Leah's statement "This time I will praise the Lord" is key in how to cooperate with this process. Pastor James Noriega put it like this: "We worshiped our way into this mess, and by God's grace, we will worship our way out."[47] The word *worship* means giving something the weight it deserves. Jesus is real— and worshiping Him means giving Him weight over the things that charm us most. It means choosing what will draw us closer to Him and avoiding the things that will draw us away.

For me, as with Leah, my spiritual growth chart zoomed when grief overwhelmed me. When my husband died, my world was so shaken that out of sheer survival I began to sing hymns to my soul each night. (In my book *The God of All Comfort*, I tell what a key part great music and its truth-filled lyrics played in helping me survive.) For two years, I sang all the verses to "Be Still My Soul" every night. I began to listen to MP3 sermons every day while I biked or got dressed and fixed my hair, grasping the truths I heard like a drowning woman gasping for air. (I especially was helped by Tim Keller's sermons from Redeemer.com because they got to the root of my problem.) I called two particularly strong Christian friends from my past, Sylvia and Ann, and asked if we could reignite our friendship. (They now come to my cabin from their respective states every year for a week of iron sharpening iron.) I got counseling from a wise Christian counselor. I read edifying books, biographies of those who made a difference because God was so real to them (such as Dietrich Bonhoeffer, Amy Carmichael, and Jonathan Edwards) and nonfiction by authors of substance (such as Philip Yancey, C. S. Lewis, and Henri Nouwen).[48] I started praying through the Psalms so that I was not just pouring out my own thoughts but using the very words of God. I spent more time outdoors, praising the wisdom of the One who covers the woods with forget-me-nots, causes the sun to take the earth by its edges, and shows the hawk how to soar.

These ordinary means of grace kept me moving toward Jesus. But there was something else, even more important: I began to gaze inwardly upon God. My mind would go to Him, thinking of Him. Even while occupied with laundry or driving to the post office, I found my mind going to God with increasing frequency. As A. W. Tozer says, "A new set of eyes (so to speak) will develop within us enabling us to be looking at God while our outward eyes are seeing the scenes of this passing world."[49] This, more than anything, brought me into His arms.

I couldn't just "stop grieving." I had to let Jesus fill that space. Again, it is repentance (I had to let go of Steve, for my desperation showed he had become too much of my hope, my solid rock) and faith (I had to set my affections on Jesus, my real life).

My senses awakened. I became more alert to God's voice and to the people who came across my path. I was worshiping, giving Jesus more and more the weight He deserves. Slowly He drew me through the icy river of grief and into His arms.

I do not want to stop. I want to be alert all day for my idols. I want Him to keep changing me. Just the other day, I told the Lord: *I have a steady, quiet stream of joy. My life still has purpose, and You are leading me in exciting ways. I never thought, without Steve, that life could be this sweet. But it is. Because of You.*

Leah suffers, but that suffering leads her into intimacy with God because she releases her idol and turns to Him. He brings her through her grief and into His arms.

GIVE ME CHILDREN OR I'LL DIE!

Ironically, it is the beloved and beautiful Rachel who is never delivered from her idols and the sorrow they bring. She dies with bitterness on her lips.

I believe Rachel's deep idol is control, and it produces rotten fruit throughout her life: wrath, envy, cruelty, stealing, deception, and despair. I don't see her in a satisfying relationship with anyone—not her husband, her sister, or her children. When she was barren, she says to Jacob, "Give me children, or I shall die!"

(Genesis 30:1). The question "What, if you lost it, would make life not worth living?" makes it easy to see Rachel's near idol. She wants sons, more than Leah has, and she does whatever she can to get them. (Family—in particular, sons, who could grow up and take care of the farm—was the idol of that culture. We are all vulnerable to our own culture's idols, whatever they are.)

Rachel pushes Jacob into the arms of her maidservant, Bilhah, and when Bilhah has sons, they got wild names that revealed Rachel's idolatry. One of them Rachel named Naphtali, which is Hebrew for "wrestlings," for she says, "I have wrestled with my sister and have prevailed" (Genesis 30:8). When Leah's son finds mandrakes (a plant thought to make women fertile), Rachel, who is definitely the one in this trio who is in control, tells her sister that she can sleep with Jacob for a night in exchange for those mandrakes. When the family is fleeing Paddan-aram, it is Rachel who steals her father's gods, hiding them under her skirt, pretending to be innocent. As Leslie Williams writes, "Without knowing fully what we are doing, we hide the things we secretly love and admire under our skirts, like Rachel, sitting primly and righteously on our camels, wondering why we are not whole, why we still suffer, why we feel unreconciled to the God we profess."[50]

Rachel spends her life in a quest for sons, blistering at Jacob, her sister, and her God about her pain. She misses the life God longed for her to have.

DON'T MISS GOD'S DREAMS FOR YOU

How *should* we respond when the door to a dream seems shut? What do we do when marriage or motherhood or physical healing seems unattainable? Do we keep knocking with bleeding knuckles? Rachel was frenetic for children all of her married life and died with bitterness on her lips. Is that the life God has called us to?

Over the last two years I have been mentoring a woman named Hope. I remember when we first started meeting and she told me, "I want a heart of flesh—a heart as soft, as tender, and as malleable as Play-Doh." I thought, *Oh, what God could do with that!*

Hope is petite and pretty, with long, dark hair and a slim, athletic body. She eats right, runs five miles a day, and studies the Word diligently. She works part-time as a secretary at a church and she's married to her best friend. They have a sweet marriage, reading, playing Scrabble, actively participating in ministry together, immersing themselves in the Word and prayer, and talking about what matters most.

Several years before I met Hope, the Stonecutter had begun to move in her life. As so often happens, He got her full attention when her world was shaken.

I am eager to tell you Hope's story—how she responded to the Lover of her soul and how He is leading her in a dance that was better than the dance she had ever imagined for her life.

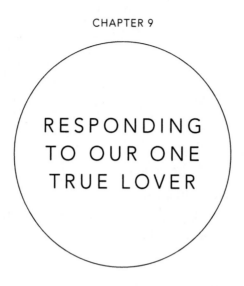

CHAPTER 9

RESPONDING
TO OUR ONE
TRUE LOVER

Arise my love, my beautiful one,
and come away.

—Song of Songs 2:13

Hope had imagined that she, like her three older sisters, would easily have children, so she was shocked when she joined the ranks of those battling infertility. She was determined to fight, to knock on the door until it opened. For years she submitted to tests and needles, praying all the time for a child.

But it didn't happen.

Hope vividly remembers the day she made a turn. She was sitting on the cold examining table once again, waiting for results. The doctor told her there was no pregnancy and new tests revealed that the likelihood of a pregnancy was decreasing. Yet her doctor was a fighter. With steel in her eyes, she looked at Hope, shook her fist in the air, and said, "I can still make a baby for you!"

Hope froze. She thought, *Is this what I look like to You, God? Angry? Shaking my fist at You?* She drove home sobbing. Releasing the dream. The last thing she wanted was to fight the One she loved with all her heart.

She resolved to be content with just her husband and herself. *After all*, she thought, *he's my best friend. We can stay up late. We can travel. . . .* Though her husband, Peter, would have liked to adopt, that path seemed too risky to Hope. She says,

> Now I understand that my fears revolved around my control idol. I would have no control over how the mother took care of herself while she was pregnant—what she would eat or drink, if she would take drugs, or if she would see a doctor. I would have no control over her will, and she might want the baby back after we'd bonded. And what about controlling love—what if I didn't love an adopted child or she didn't love me? All those fears were overwhelming.

Peter didn't pressure his wife, but he prayed that if adoption was God's plan, He would change Hope's heart.

In the Song of Songs, the first time the bridegroom comes to his bride and asks her to go higher with him, she is fearful and refuses. It feels way too risky. She wants to stay where she is, hidden in the clefts of the rock. He pleads with her, asking to see her face, but fears keep her bound. She dismisses her bridegroom, telling him to go to the mountains alone (Song of Songs 2:13–14, 17).

Hudson Taylor, a man who took enormous risks as the founder of China Inland Mission, comments on this passage: "The grieved bridegroom leaves! Poor foolish bride! She will soon find that the things that once satisfied her can satisfy her no longer. . . . Unless her love reaches the point of surrender, she will remain unsatisfied."[51]

Because Hope wanted most of all what God wanted, she asked Him to "mess with her heart" if she was wrong about adoption.

And He did.

MY UTMOST FOR HIS HIGHEST

One winter night after Christmas, Hope was reading the classic devotional *My Utmost for His Highest* by Oswald Chambers. What arrested her was Chambers's closing paragraph for that day's devotion: "Not often, but every once in a while, God brings us to a major turning point—a great crossroads in our life. From that point we either go toward a more and more slow, lazy, and useless Christian life, or we become more and more on fire, giving our utmost for His highest—our best for His glory."[52]

As Hope read that passage, she sensed God saying that she could just go on with her life, just her and Peter, and it would be okay. It wasn't sinful, but, for them, it would be "a more and more slow, lazy Christian life." Hope realized she didn't want that:

I'm not much of a risk-taker, but He enticed me. The Lover of My Soul was offering me a chance to truly glorify Him with my choice. I pondered it all night but didn't talk about it. I woke up the next morning and I was almost frustrated that God had come in and messed with my heart, even though I had asked Him to! I looked at Peter and told him God had done it: "I didn't want to want to, but I do want to adopt." As scared as I was, it was harder *not* to respond to Him.

Our God is a persistent God, never giving up on us. In the Song of Songs, the bridegroom comes back and asks again for his bride to arise and come higher up, to the "mountain of myrrh" with Him. She knows that this will mean death to her own desires, for myrrh in Scripture represents death. But now she trusts that death will lead to resurrection, and as scared as she is, she can no longer refuse him. She tells him, "I will go away to the mountain of myrrh." And the bridegroom responds, "You are altogether beautiful, my love, there is no flaw in you" (Song of Songs 4:6–7).

When I met Hope, it was years after that pivotal time in her life. She was the mother of two precious adopted children. She says confidently that this was Plan A for Peter and her all along—and that what He gave them was beyond her wildest dreams.

When we resist God, even if it seems like we are resisting for a good thing, we may actually be working at cross-purposes with Him. It is always hard to give up control, especially when it means the loss of a dream. But is it God's dream we're giving up or ours? Each of us thinks we know best, but truly, our puny wisdom is a drop of water compared to the ocean of wisdom of the great I AM.

THE PERFECT CHRISTIAN FAMILY

When I led Hope through a Bible study on idolatry, she responded like the tenderhearted person that she is. It thrilled me to see her rapid growth, to see the changes that occur when an individual recognizes her idols and turns away from them toward the Lover of her soul.

Hope, like me, identified her predominant idol to be control. Those of us with this idol often forget that what God asks of us is to be faithful and to leave the results to Him. Hope thought that creating the perfect Christian family was within her control. She's not the only one in the evangelical world to believe this lie.

How did we come to think that if we just did things "right" we would have a model family? Perhaps this illusion has come, in part, because we have heard erroneous teaching on the book of Proverbs. The book of Proverbs, like every book in the biblical canon, is divinely inspired, but we must understand its genre. A proverb is a maxim that we should follow because it leads us in the wisest path. But it is a probability, not a promise. For example, we are told:

A slack hand causes poverty,
but the hand of the diligent makes rich.

(Proverbs 10:4)

This is a maxim, which means it is generally true that the lazy person will be poor and the diligent person will have plenty. But a lazy person can win the lottery and a diligent person can have a tornado destroy his crops. That does not disprove the proverb, because a proverb is simply a probability.

As we looked at before when we considered God's use of metaphor, when we do not interpret Scripture according to its genre, we misinterpret Scripture. Yet many teachers quote proverbs as if they are in the genre of promises, and so we are disappointed in God when we experience an exception to what our Christian community may have promoted as a "promise." One of the most misunderstood verses in our Christian communities is Proverbs 22:6:

> Train up a child in the way he should go;
> even when he is old he will not depart from it.

This is generally true, but it is not a promise. In other words, a child who departs from the truth may still have been trained in the way he should go. Likewise, it is possible that if you are an excellent wife, your children and husband will rise up and call you blessed (Proverbs 31:28). But they might not. It's not up to us to decide what happens; it's up to us to be faithful.

When we think we are in control of results, rather than called to be obedient as we release the results to God, we will experience guilt, tension, and discouragement. Hope told me that as her family grew, she wanted to be the perfect Proverbs 31 wife and mother. She had a picture in her head of the perfect home, perfect meals, and perfect children: "well-behaved, obedient, and saved!" She also pictured a happy husband who was home each night enjoying it all.

"The problem," Hope told me, "was that whenever anything threatened to disrupt this perfect mental picture, I'd become resentful and angry. I was living in a constant state of striving, complaining, disappointment, depression, and exhaustion. I was driving myself, my husband, and my children crazy. I was robbing our home of joy."

Hope's negative emotions were her red flags that an idol was operating. When she recognized her idol of control—control over how her husband and children acted, how her home looked, how others saw her—she responded to the Spirit of God and laid down on His altar her desires for particular outcomes. With wonder, she told me, "If I lay down at the altar every time my children disobey me, every time my husband is late getting home or has yet another business trip, if I give all those circumstances back to God for *Him* to be in control of, then I find Life. My heart rests."

When an idol is chiseled, and the Spirit of God moves in, we see beautiful fruit come from our souls instead of rotten fruit. Hope is experiencing that:

The past several weeks I have seen a subtle difference in the way I respond to circumstances. In the past, when my husband would call to say he was going out of town again, my usual response would be to sigh and list all that his absence would cost me. Now I say, even right out loud, "It is Yours, Lord. I give it to You. You will take care of us." Now that is not me at *all!* God is also helping me lay down bigger things, like my children's salvation, always giving them back to Him as an offering of faith. And I am at peace.

Each time Hope let go of the reins of control, her True Lover came to her. He did not give her the perfect family, but He did give her peace. It is likely that when Hope's children are old they will walk in the way they have been trained, and it is likely that Hope's husband will rise up and call her blessed. But Hope is releasing all that to the One who is ultimately in control.

In this fallen world, though there are wonderful families, no one has the perfect family—not in the home and not in the church. We must be careful to find our identity in Christ rather than in creating the perfect Christian family, whatever we imagine that to be.

Madeleine L'Engle writes, "The illusion of a perfect family is another of America's golden calves."[53] L'Engle says that what God really calls us to is to love one another as the imperfect beings we are rather than blame each other for not being who we want each other to be. Isn't that the kind of Christlike grace for which each of us longs? How different our families and churches would be if we would embrace this truth!

Hope was laying down her illusion of a perfect family and living out love for her imperfect family. But before grace could flow in abundance, another stone needed to be excised.

STONEWALLING

Hope's father had been addicted to alcohol, had not loved her well, and had died of the ravages of alcoholism when she was a young mother. As she says, "I waited my whole life for him to tell me he was sorry, but the alcohol took him before that happened. I was in counseling for years but decided I'd gotten as far as I could in forgiveness. I decided that this little stone would have to remain in my heart because I had been so wounded. The scars would simply not heal." Hope had developed a habit, beginning in childhood, of dealing with the hurtful actions of others. She withdrew. It's called "stonewalling."

I think it is very common for Christians to stonewall, because it seems more benign than lashing out, name-calling, or throwing things—but it is *not* benign. It is a way of hurting others, and deep in our hearts, we know it. Counselor John Gottman talks about "the four horsemen of the apocalypse" and the danger they bring, for example, to the stability of a marriage: "Usually these four horsemen clip-clop into the heart of a marriage in the following order: criticism, contempt, defensiveness, and stonewalling."[54]

Stonewalling is deadly. In a marriage, it is the most reliable predictor of divorce because it produces an emotional divorce, with actual divorce not far behind.

Hope's marriage seemed sound, but she began to identify how her "little stone" was causing problems in many other relationships: sometimes with friends, sometimes with her mother, and sometimes with her wonderful but strong-willed daughter. She loved all these people dearly, but her stonewalling was hurting her relationships with them.

Hope came to see that her control idol told her not to let people who had offended her off the hook too easily. "How prone I was to hold a grudge, to require the offender to earn my forgiveness. I told myself, *If they are really sorry, then I'll forgive—no problem.* But I was the judge of what 'really sorry' meant, and sometimes the other person's words never met my criteria."

This was how Hope thought she could protect herself. Idols are an attempt to solve a problem, but they don't, they make it worse. Hope found herself on the other side of a tall wall she had erected, feeling bitter, angry, cold, and lonely.

As Hope told me of her destructive habit of stonewalling, I felt it was time to confess my past, my own stonewalling, and how God broke through.

When we adopted our daughter Beth, she came to us broken and wounded. Her arm had been severed as a baby, then she'd been abandoned, and then she'd grown up in a Bangkok orphanage with wounded caretakers who hurt her emotionally and physically. Beth had retreated behind a thick wall. At the age of twelve, when we adopted her, she had trouble respond-ing to *anyone.* Even though I knew in my head that it was what counselors call "attachment disorder," I still was hurt by her repeated unresponsiveness to any kindness. In time, I found myself withdrawing instead of moving toward her. One day I lashed out at her: "I know you don't love me!" She stared at me and retreated to her room. I was only exacerbating her fears that I, like all her caregivers in the past, would love her poorly.

In contrast, I watched my husband give Beth grace upon grace, continuing to press in even when he received no response. He did puzzles, watched endless *Road Runner* cartoons, and played basketball—all ways to enter into her world. She started wandering into his den, just standing there silently, rocking on her heels. He recognized that she was moving toward him. He'd swivel his chair around, close his book, and ask her what she'd like to do. "Basketball? *Road Runner?*" More and more, like a frozen bud opens to the warm sun, Beth began to open to her dad.

At Steve's funeral, all our children spoke, but when Beth tried, she broke down, shaking her head, retreating down from the platform with tears rolling down her cheeks. (How different she was from the emotionless child we had adopted!) Her older sister Sally jumped up, met her on the steps, and led her back to the mike, whispering to her that she *could* do it. Then Sally asked the congregation of a thousand to just give her sister a minute. Beth finally spoke brokenly, hushing the house.

Dad . . . loved me. [Long pause and tears.] He always took time . . . always put down whatever he was doing. . . . I liked it when Mom had to speak on a weekend so I could have him to myself. [The congregation roared.] He'd take me to the movies and we'd eat popcorn and jelly beans. A father and a daughter. . . . He loved me. Now he can have all the jelly beans he wants. [More laughter. Beth blew her nose, and finally Sally let her sit down. The congregation broke out into applause.]

As I later told Hope, I sat at the funeral that day praying, *Oh Lord, give me the grace that Steve had, that I can love my daughter well.* And God has helped me to do that, to keep loving even when Beth withdraws. Beth is healing. Grace *is* amazing—not just because it's unnatural, but because it heals like nothing else.

One of the themes I see in the Song of Songs is how much grace the bridegroom gives the bride. She is unsure of herself, doesn't even want him to look at her (Song of Songs 1:6). But he gives her grace upon grace, seeing her as the beautiful bride she will become, continually praising her, moving toward her, and loving her. This is also our Lover, our Friend—and we are to be like Him in loving one another.

Beth was broken, but in truth, we are *all* broken people. We all need grace. We all long for others to keep on keeping on, even when we let them down, even when we are our *most* difficult. How we need to learn to give grace, as He has given to us. "Grace," I said to Hope, "is the opposite of stonewalling."

ALWAYS OUR MOVE

I asked Hope to study several passages on grace and also suggested reading Philip Yancey's classic, *What's So Amazing About Grace?* The first thing that impressed her was that true forgiveness always demands suffering. It hurts to forgive someone who doesn't deserve to be forgiven. Someone *must* pay the debt. It's what Christ had to do for us. This insight was the beginning of Hope forgiving her father.

Then, when Hope listened to a sermon on forgiveness by Tim Keller, she was struck by one point. Keller says that when there is a distance between us and another person, it is *always* our move. As Hope told me, "It was the last thing that I wanted to hear, but that sermon has changed my actions nearly every day since. Instead of sulking, I must move toward the person—

in doing so, I am moving away from my control idol and toward God."

Do you see what Hope was seeing? You cannot just stop a negative behavior (such as withdrawing), you must start a positive behavior (moving toward the person who hurt you). The only way you can do that is to believe that God will be there for you. It requires repentance *and* faith.

One day Hope's strong-willed daughter had pushed the boundaries all day long. Hope finally sent her to her room. In the past, she would have waited for her daughter to come down and apologize. Instead, she found herself climbing the stairs to her daughter. Her daughter turned over on the bed, toward her mother, her face wary. But instead of anger, she saw tenderness. Hope said, "Honey, let's go out for ice cream." (This was huge for Hope, who is very cautious about giving her children sugar!) And off they went, her daughter astounded. While licking her cone of Rocky Road, chock-full of sugar, chocolate, nuts, and marshmallows, she asked, "Mama, why would you take me here after *everything* I did today?"

Hope scooped her up in her arms and told her it was because her love for her was absolutely unconditional. She didn't have to earn it—she would always have it. Contemplatively, she told me later, "The more I start in some tiny way to *get* the gospel, the more I can give it to others."

This is gospel transformation. This is the power from on high that removes our stones and puts flesh in their place. This is grace.

ARISE, MY LOVE

The better we understand the gospel and the depth of Christ's love for us, the more willing we will be to turn from our idols and run to Him. He is waiting with open arms, for His "love is better than wine," His "name is oil poured out," and His banner over us is love (Song of Songs 1:2–3; 2:4). And amazingly, when we go through trials, when our dreams shatter, our intimacy with the Lord actually increases. In the close of the Song of Songs, we see a transformed bride and this tender verse: "Who is that coming up from the wilderness, leaning on her beloved?" (8:5).

Depending on idols is always an attempt to solve a problem. They promise to be our saviors, but they cannot be. In the final story I am going to tell you, the woman who cleaned for me and I were each tempted to be our own saviors in different ways, but the solution to our heart problem was the same. We needed to behold the beauty of the gospel so that we could arise, leave our idols, and follow Him.

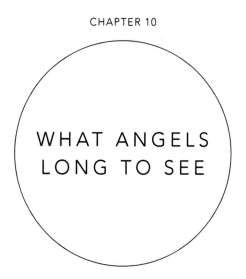

CHAPTER 10

WHAT ANGELS
LONG TO SEE

Angels love to look into the gospel. They never get tired of it. So what does that mean? It means gospel ministry is endlessly creative. . . . The gospel is not the ABC's of Christianity, it's A to Z. . . . The gospel is pretty much the solution to every problem.

—Tim Keller, "The Gospel-Driven Church"

I had just moved to Kansas City to spend the winter months near my son John and his wife and their six children. I was visiting churches. A woman at one of those churches heard I was looking for help with cleaning and asked me to consider her daughter, whom I will call Nicki. She said, "Nicki doesn't know the Lord. She's living with a not-so-good boyfriend. But there's a spiritual hunger in her, and I'd be so thankful if she could get to know you. She's a hard worker and she would do a good job cleaning for you."

Though hesitant, I agreed to meet Nicki for an interview. She drove to my house in a car with such a loud rumble that I could hear her approaching when she was a block away. I opened the door to a rail-thin young woman who was already talking rapidly, pleading her case. "I'm Nicki and I'm a hard worker. I'd do a really good job for you."

I smiled and asked her to come in and sit down. I gestured for her to hang her sweatshirt in the closet so I wouldn't interrupt her continual stream of talk: "My boyfriend got laid off a year ago, and then I got laid off, and we really need money 'cause it's really hard. I have two other cleaning jobs, and if I could work for you, too, I think we might maybe get by for now. I'd do a really good job for you. I know how to clean, I do, and I hope you'll let me clean for you. His mother lives with us and she's disabled, so we are really having a hard time, so I hope you'll give me a chance, and I'll show you I'm a good worker and you won't be sorry you hired me. In fact, if you want me to start today, I got some cleaning stuff right in the car, and that would be good 'cause we're really having a hard time, and then you could see that I'll do a good job. . . . " She paused, and we both took a breath! Her eyes were big, pleading.

"Okay, Nicki," I told her, "let's give it a try today."

She jumped up, ran to her car, got her supplies, and put all that nervous energy to work scrubbing down my kitchen and bathrooms. She *did* do a good job, but when I got out my checkbook, she said, "Dee, do you think you could pay me in cash? That would really help us."

"Nicki, usually people want to do that so that they don't have to report it to the IRS. And that's not legal. I need to pay you by check."

"Oh, it's not that. It's just that things are kind of a mess at our bank and we need to get that sorted out."

Again, I was uneasy. I told her I could pay her in cash legally for a few times, but it couldn't be long term. She agreed and said she'd figure something out.

But a month later, when I tried again to pay her by check, she said, "I didn't really tell you the truth, Dee, and I'm sorry. But a few years ago, times were really tough and I passed some bad checks. Nothing happened, but I've been afraid. I don't want to renew my driver's license or pay taxes, because then they might find out I'm still around and come after me. Will you help me? I really need the money, but if you pay me by check, I could get in a lot of trouble."

I thought, *Oh, girl, you are really walking on thin ice by not paying taxes and driving without a license.* I knew she couldn't keep hiding and I couldn't be her accomplice. I didn't even know where to begin to help her, but I paid her in cash and told her I'd talk to some people and figure out a plan of action.

A few days later, I got a call from Nicki, who was sobbing hysterically. This was our conversation as I remember it:

"Dee, you gotta help me. I'm so scared."

"What's going on?"

"I would never steal from you, Dee. You've been so good to me."

"But you stole from someone?"

Nicki continued sobbing. "I took some jewelry from the other women I clean for and sold the stuff at a truck stop. I got just enough to get us by. I didn't know their stuff was worth so much. One of them says one ring was worth twenty-five thousand dollars."

"Oh, Nicki."

"That lady had a security camera, and it has a movie of me taking her jewelry. She's pressing charges. Dee, do you think I'll go to jail? I just can't go to jail. I'm so scared. I didn't know it was worth all that money, but she's got a heart like ice. You gotta help me, Dee. You got a good heart. Help me, Dee."

"Oh, Nicki. I'll see what I can do. I need to talk to a lawyer."

"You gotta help me, Dee."

"I'll try."

I hung up and put my head between my hands. This was real trouble. Then I had the thought, *Maybe she stole from me too.* All I had of material value from Steve were four pieces of emerald jewelry: an engagement ring, a pendant he'd given me for our fifteenth anniversary, a bracelet for our twenty-fifth, and earrings on his last Christmas. I was wearing the ring. But were the other three pieces still safely in my jewelry box? I bolted for the bedroom. They weren't in the top part of the velvet-lined box—maybe I'd hidden them in the secret compartment. No. Empty. *And where was my mother's ruby ring? And my late mother-in-law's wedding ring?* My thoughts raced, denial rising to protect my grieving heart: *Nicki said she didn't steal from me. Maybe I put them someplace else.* But then I also thought, *Nicki has lied to me before. And where else would I have put them?*

In my heart of hearts, I knew she had taken them, but I was reluctant to face it.

I stood in front of my plundered jewelry box with racing thoughts and emotions. Forgiveness always demands a price. Somebody has to pay when a wrong is done, and it hurts to pay. Angry thoughts multiplied. *How could she do this to me? I've tried to bless her. Did she not even think how much Steve's gifts would mean to me now that he is gone?* I could almost feel my heart hardening.

My control idol was whispering to me that God might not deal with Nicki the way she should be dealt with. I was having emotions similar to those of Jonah when he told God that he knew God was gracious and would let those terrible Ninevites off the hook (Jonah 4:2–3)! I didn't want to give up control to such a merciful God. I wanted Nicki to hurt as I had been hurt. I wanted to forget the Lord, what He did for me, how He absorbed the pain for me, and exact a pound of flesh from Nicki by refusing to forgive her and help her. I wanted to forget the gospel.

Help me, Lord.

A scene from *Les Misérables* flashed in my head. Jean Valjean had spent nineteen years in prison because he stole bread for his family. His treatment in prison was harsh and his heart grew hard. When he finally got out, a kindhearted bishop offered him food and shelter in his home. Before dawn, Jean Valjean arose, stole the bishop's silver spoons and forks, and fled. Constables caught him and brought him to the bishop, exposing his deceit. But the bishop looked at Valjean and said, "Ah! Here you are! . . . I am glad to see you. Well, but how is this? I gave you the candlesticks too, which are of silver like the rest, and for which you can certainly get two hundred francs. Why did you not carry them away with your forks and spoons?"[55]

Surprised, the constables let Valjean go. Even though Valjean had wronged the bishop, the bishop forgave him and suffered the loss willingly. Why?

Because of the gospel. Because he knew how he had been forgiven and therefore could not refuse to forgive.

I blistered. I didn't want to forgive. I felt as Hope had— almost mad at God for messing with my heart, even though I had asked Him to help me. It hurt when He brought that scene from *Les Misérables* to my memory, and my flesh battled with His Spirit. I remember saying, "Okay, Lord, I forgive." But I forgave in my head, not my heart.

Just a few days later I started receiving collect calls from the jail where Nicki was being held. She tearfully pleaded with me to pay her bail. *I'm so scared, Dee. You gotta help me get out of here.* After the sixth or seventh call, I phoned a friend with whom I'd done jail ministry. I told her the situation and asked her what I should do.

She told me, "Nicki is exactly where God wants her to be. This is in her best interest. I've seen so many women in jail come to their senses and turn to God. You can visit her, send her Bible studies—but don't pay her bail. Whatever time she serves now while waiting for her court date will be applied to her sentence."

I mailed Nicki a Bible and several Bible studies, but I didn't visit her during the two months she was in jail. I told myself I was busy traveling—and I was. But the real reason I didn't go to see her was that I was withholding full forgiveness. What we often do instead of completely surrendering our idols is "manage" our idols. I would send her Bible studies but not visit her. It's like the man who stops engaging in adultery but still clings to his idol by looking at pornography. He tells himself this isn't as bad, but he's being deceived, because the beast is still prowling in the cage with him. As long as I didn't fully forgive Nicki from my heart, the beast was still in the cage with me.

Nicki wrote me, thanking me profusely for sending me the materials: "Dee, I'm reading the Bible all the time and doing all the studies. Please send me more. I need them so much."

My ice melted a little.

At Nicki's court date they released her without any further penalty. She called me as soon as she got out, and I asked her to come to the house. When I opened the door, she was already in tears. I hugged her, took her coat, and had her sit down. I said, "Nicki, I have to ask you something. Did you steal from me?"

Tears sprang forth. Between sobs she said, "I'm so sorry. I wish I could get them back, but I sold them at a truck stop. I'm so sorry, Dee."

I began to cry too. My tears were for my treasures lost. Steve's gifts were truly beyond recovering. And yet even as I grieved their loss, I knew what he would say: "In light of eternity, what's important here, honey?" Nicki was watching me. A soul in need of grace.

What happened next was almost like a dream. I had such a sense of the presence of God descending, of being led in a slow dance. My actions and my words were not really from me at all. It was God's grace flowing through me, for I don't think I had it yet to give.

I took two folding chairs and placed them in front of my framed print of Rembrandt's *The Return of the Prodigal Son*. My former assistant, Christy, had bought it, framed it, and presented it to me as a housewarming gift. She'd heard me gush about it, listened to me as I read aloud to her from Henri Nouwen's book of the same title. Nouwen tells when this painting first seized his heart:

> One day I went to visit my friend Simone Landrien in the community's small documentation center. As we spoke, my eyes fell on a large poster pinned on her door. I saw a man in a great red cloak tenderly touching the shoulders of a disheveled boy kneeling before him. I could not take my eyes away. I felt drawn by the intimacy between the two figures, the warm red of the man's cloak, the golden yellow of the boy's tunic, and the mysterious light engulfing them both.[56]

I asked Nicki to come and sit down with me in front of this painting. She came quickly and sat down, crossing one long, thin leg over another, gazing at the vibrant colors in the painting. We sat in silence, absorbing the portrait. It's such a picture of the gospel—and whenever I look at it, the layer of ice that keeps forming over my soul melts. The circle of light around the father embracing his broken son. The servants, amazed at the father's love. The older son up on the step in the shadows, arms crossed, oozing anger and bitterness.

I told her I was going to tell her the story, because this was really a story about her, about me, and about God, who loves us both.[57]

"We are all in this painting," I said. "This father you see in the red cloak had two sons. The father loved both of his sons so much, but neither one loved him. They just wanted what they could get from him. The father was rich, and the younger son was eager for him to die so he could get his inheritance. One day he asked the father to give him his inheritance early, and though the father was sad, he gave it to him. Then this younger son went to a far country and squandered it all in riotous living. When all the money was gone, the younger son had to work feeding pigs and wished he could have some of their food, for he was hungry. At that point Jesus tells us he came to his senses."

Nicki looked at me, tears filling her eyes. I rubbed her back as she stared at the portrait. I continued with the story.

"The younger son decides to go home to his father and tell him how sorry he is. He realizes how he has hurt his father. He walks home, planning his speech of repentance. He is going to tell his father that he is no longer worthy to be called his son but to please give him a job as a hired servant. But Nicki, the boy never got to give his speech."

"Why not?"

"Because the father had been watching for him, hoping he would return. And when he saw him, a long way off, he ran to him, embracing him, kissing him. Then he cried out to his servants: 'Bring quickly the best robe and put it on him, and put a ring on his hand, and shoes on his feet. And bring the fattened calf and kill it, and let us eat and celebrate. For this my son was dead and is alive again; he was lost, and is found.'"

Now tears were streaming down Nicki's cheeks.

"Do you see yourself in this painting, Nicki?"

Hesitantly, she pointed to the younger son, kneeling before the father.

"Yes. When I opened my door to you this morning, I could see that you were broken, like this son. And just like that father ran to his son, God is running to you. He longs to forgive you, to make you His child. Even though you hurt people and you hurt God, He forgives you. In fact, He paid for your sin. Do you know how?"

"On the cross."

"Yes."

"Nicki, would you like to tell Him you are sorry now? Are you willing to surrender your life to Him?"

"That's what I want to do, Dee."

"You can do it right here, right now. Just tell Him how you feel, and thank Him for dying for you. Ask Him to come into your heart and change you."

"I need that so bad. I need Him to help me 'cause I have these sticky fingers and I can't seem to stop them from taking things."

My heart leapt. She didn't want to be delivered just from sin's penalty but also from its power.

"He can help you. He came to rescue us not only from hell but from sticky fingers and all kinds of other things."

Together we prayed. Together we wept. I hugged her, and I meant it. But I knew the story was not over.

"Nicki, there is more to this story, and I need to tell you the rest. Because I'm in this painting too."

"You are like the father," Nicki said.

"I want to be, Nicki, and I'm feeling more like that this morning, but for the past two months I've been much more like this man." I pointed to a man with a stony face standing outside the circle of light, up on a step, reeking of anger. His body language waved the red flags of idolatry, of control, of unwillingness to forgive his brother.

"This is the older son. He didn't love the father either. His father is so happy to have his younger brother home, but this son cannot enter into the joy of his father. He can't forgive. He's miserable and angry. His father entreats him, but he disrespectfully says to his father, 'Look! All these years I've been slaving for you, and I never disobeyed your orders. Yet you never even gave me a young goat so I could celebrate with my friends. But when this son of yours who has squandered your property with prostitutes comes home, you kill the fattened calf for him!'

"Nicki, I have been like this older son. I forgave you in my head, but my heart was still hard. Even though I sent you Bible studies and wrote you, I was too angry to visit you. I was wrong. God has forgiven me so much that I had no right to withhold my forgiveness to you. Jesus went all the way to the cross to pay for my sin. I do forgive you, from my heart, and I'm sorry it took so long. I need you to forgive me for my icy heart."

"Oh, Dee. I'm so sorry I hurt you."

"And you forgive me?"

She nodded, weeping. I reached for her and she for me. Hugging and weeping beneath Rembrandt's portrait of the gospel.

Before God did this mighty work in my heart, showing me my root problem of idolatry, I was in the company of Christians who thought of the gospel as the way to get into Christianity, as the way to be freed from the *penalty* of sin. I didn't realize the gospel was also the way to be freed from the *power* of sin.

But it is.

Idols are how we replace God. Peering into the gospel is how we replace idols.

Peering into the richness of the gospel, as Peter tells us angels long to do (1 Peter 1:12), can help us have the faith to open our hearts to God and let Him replace our idols with Himself. Then He moves in and sets us free from the chains of our idols.

It's been two years and Nicki has been faithful in going to church with her mother. The last time I saw her, I asked her if she was still living with her boyfriend, and she was. She said, "I need to get myself right before I move out." She's managing her idol instead of surrendering it, but I know we all have that tendency. We are still so vulnerable to believing the lies of the enemy: *Jesus won't be enough. He doesn't love You that much. He won't do what is best for You.*

Yet the more we know Him, the more we see Him as He really is, the more the truth of the gospel defeats the enemy.

As we spend time with Him, as we go to Him in our minds and hearts, He comes. He confides His secrets, as Psalm 25:14 tells us, in those who are intimate with Him, bringing them higher up and deeper in. We find we are able to unclasp our hands from the treasures of this world, for we have something so much better.

HEART OF FLESH

I began this book telling you how a fresh look at Martha of Bethany and *her* problem of idolatry helped me to see my own. It seems fitting, therefore, to close with these sisters, and to see how any idols of their hearts lay as broken as Mary's famous alabaster jar. The expulsive love of a new affection pushed out idols of control, comfort, or approval.

The crucifixion is less than a week away. Somehow Mary knows. Perhaps Martha does too. And oh, they are grieved. Can you even imagine? So when Mary enters the room with a bottle holding, most likely, their family savings in the form of perfume, Martha does not jump up to control her little sister. She is quietly supportive.

When Mary breaks the bottle, pouring out the provision that could have made them quite comfortable and secure, again, Martha stands by her sister.

When Mary pulls her hair clasp out so that her hair tumbles down, there are gasps. This was something no Jewish woman should do in public. As Mary wipes her Lord's feet with her hair, everyone is rebuking her. Everyone except Martha. But the harsh scolding from others doesn't matter—only one opinion matters to Mary. And Jesus makes that very clear, not just by the look in His eyes, but by silencing the disciples and saying this sacrifice will always be remembered, wherever the gospel is preached.

These sisters only care about Jesus. I like to think that as He suffered those long six hours on the cross, their fragrance still clung to Him, comforting Him.

It is love that expels their idols. They *know* they had everything they needed in Him.

And so do we.

CONTINUING THE JOURNEY

By now, you have probably identified one or more of your idols, and this is huge. Before we identify our idols we are not even in a battle. Our eyes are shut and we are easy prey to the enemy. Now it is time to continue this journey of being released from the power of sin through the combustion cycle of repentance and faith.

Every time something bad comes out of your mouth or your life, ask yourself: *What is the idol lie I am believing?* Recognize it and repent, knowing your idol will put up a fight, continuing to spew out lies. There will be pain in turning away, but so much greater pain if you give in. And remember this: every death leads to a glorious resurrection. After the "mountain of myrrh," after the winter of death, comes *life*, comes a glorious spring. So turn, and behold the Lover of your Soul, who is the Truth. He is standing with open arms calling to you:

> "Arise, my love, my beautiful one,
>   and come away . . . "
>
> (Song of Songs 2:10)

Don't look back, don't take your eyes off Him, but run, right into the shelter of His arms.

Bible Study and Discussion Guide

LEADER'S NOTES BEGIN ON PAGE 245.

Welcome! The following guide is designed to be used alongside each chapter of *Idol Lies*. My own life and the lives of women piloting this study have been so dramatically changed by understanding our heart idols that I am excited about what God will do in your life. I encourage you to do this study with a friend or group of women if possible, for women meeting together, seeking God, sharing honestly, and caring for one another is one of the sweetest places this side of heaven.

What *you* bring to this gathering is a huge factor in how rich your group will be. Here are a few things to keep in mind as you begin.

- The women who are most likely to form deep friendships with each other and with God are the women who show they care through being faithful in attendance and in homework.

- The homework is divided into five days. Work through these questions before you meet with your group. When you meet, you will first watch a short video and then discuss your homework.

- The guide is designed for you to do the first lesson before the first meeting.

- You could write in this book or, if you need more space, you could use a separate notebook. You could also go to **http://worthypublishing.com/books/Idol-Lies/** to download and print the lesson. The downloadable format will provide extra space and also has links for valuable extra resources—all of it intended to allow you to more effectively absorb and apply Scripture's truths in your life.

- Something else to keep in mind when you meet: If you are naturally talkative, hold back to give the shy women a chance to gather courage and speak up. And if you are shy, circle a few answers ahead of time and ask the Lord for strength to speak up so you too can enrich the group.

- As you begin your journey into *Idol Lies* you may also want to check out the *free* Dee Brestin Ministries app for your iPad, iPod, iPhone, or Droid phone as well as our accompanying teaching DVDs. Find out more at DeeBrestin.com/idol-lies/.

Take the above to heart, and this will be an unforgettable group.

—Dee Brestin

LESSON 1:
LAYERS OF LIES

VIDEO 1: Layers of Lies (The videos before each lesson are ten to twenty minutes each and available at **http://worthypublishing .com/books/Idol-Lies/**. You can watch them on your own or wait and watch them in your group. For more information on the videos, see the leader's notes starting on page 245.)

ICE BREAKERS

A. Share your name, why you've come, and what you hope to receive from this study.
B. What stood out to you from the video and why?

——————

Prepare your heart for homework each day with prayer and music.

——————

PERSONAL PRAYER: Combining prayer and Scripture leads to power. When a verse in the study becomes "radioactive" to you, use it for personal prayer. For example, this week one of the first scriptures is Jeremiah 17:9, which says we have deceitful hearts. Right then you could pray, "Lord, help me see the truth about my real desires and give me Your desires instead." This is a life-changing way to combine Bible study and prayer.

SONG: Sing to the Lord with understanding. Suggestions for this week: "Open the Eyes of My Heart" by Paul Baloche, "Eyes Wide Open" by Sara Groves, and "When I Survey the Wondrous Cross" by Isaac Watts. If you Google these titles and artists you will find various websites with lyrics, music, or video versions.

DAY 1:
DECEITFUL HEARTS

1. Read chapter 1 in the book, underlining or highlighting ideas, phrases, or verses that stand out to you.

    A. Jeremiah 17:9 says, "The heart is deceitful above all things." How, in the story in this chapter about Dee's assistants, had Dee deceived herself?

    B. Proverbs 20:5 says, "The purpose in a man's heart is like deep water, but a man of understanding will draw it out." How did Dee's friend Jan begin to do that for Dee?

    C. Find at least two things that stood out to you from this chapter and explain why they stood out.

    D. A group can only be as rich as its individual members. How do you think the Lord would have you enrich this group by your:
       1) Preparation?

       2) Sharing in discussion?

3) Responding to others?

4) Openness to God?

DAY 2:
IDOLS OF THE HEART

Often we think idolatry doesn't apply to us because we confine it to outward idolatry, bowing down to statues. But the Bible also warns against inward idolatry.

If possible, watch the three-minute video from David Powlison that asks, "Is idolatry a problem in my life?"; http://www.ccef.org/video/idolatry-problem-my-life.

2. Read Ezekiel 14:1–5.
   A. When certain elders of Israel came before Ezekiel, what did God tell the prophet about their hearts?

   B. The NLT translates verse 3a as, "Son of man, these leaders have set up idols in their hearts. They have embraced things that will make them fall into sin." Explain how an idol of the heart, such as power or the approval of others, could lure a person, even a spiritual leader, into sin.

   C. Look at verse 5 and explain what idols of the heart do to our relationship with God.

3. Dr. David Powlison says that whenever something bad comes out of our mouth or our life, it reflects an idol of the heart. Can you give an example of this from your life recently?

DAY 3:
RED FLAGS FOR IDOLATRY

There is always a danger with a familiar story that we will presume we know the point when we might not. Try to put aside your presuppositions as you read.

4. Read Luke 10:38–42.
  A. Why do you think Martha was so anxious and worried?

  B. Look again at verse 40. The Greek word translated *distracted, cumbered,* or *worried* comes from a root that means "to carry a weight." Being alert to our body language is one way to become aware when a heart idol is motivating us. What do you imagine Martha's body language might have been at this time?

Anxiety is always a red flag for a heart idol. In Psalm 42, the psalmist keeps asking his soul, "Why are you cast down, O my soul, and why are you in turmoil within me?" He knows that his soul had put its trust in something other than God, which is, indeed, idolatry. So he keeps telling his soul, "Put your hope in God."

C. Two signs of manipulation are trying to invoke guilt and giving an unreasonable order. How do you see these two signs in Martha in verse 40?

D. When there is a problem in horizontal relationships, it is a red flag that there is a problem in our vertical relationship with God. What problems do you see in Martha's relationship with both Jesus and Mary?

5. When Jesus says a name twice, it is indicative of passion. In each of the following, someone Jesus loved was in danger. What danger in each of the following situations might have invoked the passion we see in Jesus?
   A. Luke 13:34

   B. Luke 22:31

   C. Luke 10:41

6. Watch yourself for the red flags of tense body language or trouble in relationships today and the rest of the week. When you are aware of a red flag, ask yourself what you are loving or trusting more than God. Record what happens here.

DAY 4:
DISCERNING WHAT WE MIGHT LOVE MORE THAN GOD

Once you spot the red flags that an idol is operating in your life, the next step is discerning what heart idol is operating. Though this is not a comprehensive list of what we might idolize, it provides a helpful way to think of our most common idols:

- Comfort/Security
- Approval/Affirmation
- Power/Control

7. Martin Luther commented that breaking commandments two through nine of the Ten Commandments is always preceded by breaking the first commandment to have no other gods before God. Give an example of how you have seen this to be true in your own life. (See Exodus 20:1–17 for the Ten Commandments.)

8. What did Jesus say to Martha in Luke 10:42? Based on Mark 12:29–30, what do you think is "the most important thing" or "the one thing that is necessary"?

9. What might have been Martha's deep heart idol that was producing bad fruit in her life? Why do you think that? Might there have been more than one idol involved? Explain.

10. How could Jesus have met Martha's needs better than her heart idol could?

11. Answer these questions to see if you can begin to discern what things might be more important to you than God.
    A. Where do you tend to go for joy and peace in your mind?

    B. What, if you lost it, might make you feel like life was not worth living?

    C. Where do you spend your money most effortlessly?

12. With these things in mind, do you have a sense of what heart idol might be prominent in your life? If so, what is it?

DAY 5:
MARTHA, MARTHA

Jesus was passionate in His conversation with Martha because idols cause pain and block intimacy with Him.

13. How was Martha's idol hurting her and keeping her from Jesus?

14. If Martha had only tried to fix the symptom (the visible sin of worry), what might have been her approach? Why is seeing the root problem (the invisible deep idol) a more effective approach?

15. Are you seeing this story differently than you have in the past? If so, explain.

16. What is your take-away from this week and why?

GROUP PRAYER: For this first meeting, the facilitator will close in prayer. If this is a group more comfortable with audible prayer, each woman can pray for the woman on her right for her understanding of this study. If group prayer is new to her, she can simply say, "Lord, bless (her name)."

———

LESSON 2:
SPIRITUAL BLINDNESS

VIDEO 2: Spiritual Blindness (available at **http://worthypublishing .com/books/Idol-Lies/**)

ICE BREAKERS

A. Think about a time in your past when you were very upset about something—such as a relationship, a rejection, or a bad grade—and now your distress seems out of proportion to what the situation deserved. What was it, how did you feel, and what might your reaction have revealed about an idol of your heart?

B. What stood out to you from the video and why?

———

Prepare your heart for homework each day with prayer and music.

———

PERSONAL PRAYER: This week pray through the verses listed in question 3 designed to help you know your heart. Ask yourself: *Who do I really love? Fear? Trust?* Ask God to help you love, fear, and trust Him.

SONG: Sing to the Lord with understanding. Suggestions for this week: The traditional version of John Newton's "Amazing Grace" or Chris Tomlin's contemporary version.

———

DAY 1:
CHRISTY, CHRISTY

1. Read chapter 2 of the book, underlining or highlighting as you go.

   A. What were some of the physical symptoms in Christy's life that evidenced idolatry?

   B. How did Christy's counselor help her see the truth?

C. What did Christy believe her deep heart idol was and how did she get free?

D. What else stood out to you in this chapter and why? Could you relate to Christy's story? If so, how?

DAY 2:
BONDAGE HAS LAYERS

When the Israelites were delivered out of external slavery, they rejoiced. Yet they had a deeper bondage, an internal slavery, that kept them grumbling and wandering in the wilderness. Our bondage has layers.

2. Read Mark 8:22–26.
   A. After Jesus touched the blind man the first time, how did the man respond to the question Jesus asked?

   B. Jesus could have healed this man with one touch, but this miracle is also a parable. What does it teach us about spiritual blindness? What does it remind us about how we see people?

3. Counselor David Powlison suggests this exercise to help you discover your heart idols. Look up the following verses and turn their commands on their heads to help discover your heart idols:

A. "You shall love the LORD your God . . ." (Deuteronomy 6:5). What do you really love, cherish? To what or whom does your mind and heart run?

B. "Trust in the LORD with all your heart . . ." (Proverbs 3:5). What do you really trust—where do you run for refuge?

C. "Those who seek the LORD lack no good thing . . . " (Psalm 34:10). What do you most frequently seek?

D. "The fear of the LORD is clean, enduring forever . . . " (Psalm 19:9). What do you fear? What, if you lost it, would make you feel desperate?

DAY 3:
TURNING GIFTS INTO GODS

The Greek word *epithumia* (inordinate desire) turns up repeatedly in the Bible to describe our tendency toward wanting something too much because we think it will satisfy our soul. The gift itself is good— it is the "over" or "lustful" desire in our hearts for the gift that snares us.

4. In each of the following verses, a gift has been turned into a "god" because it was desired "too much." (The NIV uses the phrase "too much," while other translations have the concept of an inordinate desire.) Look up the verses below and

describe the danger in each case. Also, in each example, what do you think may have been the deep heart idol that *enticed* the abuse?

A. Proverbs 20:19 (too much talk)

B. Proverbs 23:20 (too much wine, too much meat)

C. Proverbs 25:16 (too much honey)

D. Proverbs 25:17 (too much visiting)

E. Proverbs 30:8–9 (too much money)

Epithumia *may also be translated "lusts," and that sexual connotation shows what a strong pull it can have on us. In fact, James takes this word and expands it into a sexual metaphor: "The temptation to give in to evil comes from us and only us. We have no one to blame but the leering, seducing flare-up of our own lust. Lust gets pregnant, and has a baby: sin! Sin grows up to adulthood, and becomes a real killer" (James 1:14-15, MSG).*

5. Meditate on the above verse in *The Message* or another translation and unpack the metaphor:
   A. From where does temptation come and how is it described?

B. What points does Paul make by comparing it to lust or to sexual desire?

C. When that desire grabs what it thinks it must have, to what does it "give birth"?

D. Then, what does sin do?

E. Now paint this picture with an actual scenario, using a good gift like sweets or money or friendship. How could *epithumia* lure you into danger, give birth to sin, and then continue to multiply death in your own life?

DAY 4:
PUT OFF THE OLD, PUT ON THE NEW

Whenever the theme of heart transformation comes up in the Bible, you will find an exhortation to put off these inordinate desires and put on Christ. Idols cannot be removed, they can only be replaced, for our souls are like hungry whirlpools that will not tolerate a void. When we mentally replace trusting our *invisible* heart idol with trusting Christ, we are then empowered to replace the visible destructive behavior (such as saying unkind words) with visible constructive behavior (such as saying edifying words).

6. Read the appeal to believers in Ephesians 4:20–24 to be delivered from the power of sin. The word *epithumia*

occurs at the close of verse 22. How is it translated in the Bible version you're reading and what does this tell you?

7. Colossians 3 also deals with *epithumia* and replacing our heart idols with Christ: putting off and putting on. Read Colossians 3:1–4.

A. In verses 1–4, what commands are we given and why?

B. In terms of relationships, what happens to a friendship when that friend is "your life"? To a child when that child is "your life"? What happens to you in either of those cases?

C. If there comes a day when Christ is all you have, do you think you could survive? Be content? Why or why not?

DAY 5:
IDOLS DEMAND A SACRIFICE

Our idols are not our friends—they only pretend to be. They promise to solve a problem, but then they trap us. Pagans gave literal sacrifices to their idols, even sacrificing their children on the fire to the god Molech. Today, our soul idols extract blood from us as well: our health, our contentment, and our very lives.

8. Read 1 Corinthians 10:1–20.

A. What happened to *most* of the Israelites whom God had set free from slavery in Egypt (verse 5)?

B. Why are these incidents recorded for us (verses 6–7)?

C. Resisting temptation involves *enduring* suffering but then leads to freedom and peace in the arms of our Savior. What promise do we have when we are tempted by an idol (verse 13)?

D. There is a demonic element to which we open ourselves when we worship idols. Find the warning in verse 20.

9. If you are beginning to see one of your heart idols, what sacrifice do you see it might demand?

10. Read Genesis 4:1–7.
   A. What happened and why do you think Cain was so angry?

   B. When something bad comes out of our heart or mouth, it is evidence that an idol of the heart is operating. What do you think Cain's deep idol might have been and why?

C. God gave Cain a vivid word picture of the desire that could lure him into destruction. Find it in verse 7.

The New American Standard version translates verse 7 as: "If you do well, will not your countenance be lifted up?" When we embrace our idols, it shuts God out. When we turn away from them, He comes to us, His face shines upon us, and indeed, we are lifted up. God provided a way of escape for Cain, but Cain did not take it.

11. Read Genesis 4:8–16.
   A. What did Cain do, and how do you see this leading to a downward spiral?

   B. What price did Cain's idol, whatever it was, extract from him?

12. What is your take-away from this week and why?

GROUP PRAYER: Have each woman share what idol or idols she is beginning to glimpse in her own heart. Then the facilitator should lift up each woman's name and two or three women may say a sentence prayer for her before the next woman's name is lifted up. If your group is large, divide into smaller groups of three or four.

LESSON 3:
WHY ONLY SOME WILL BE SET FREE

VIDEO 3: Why Only Some Will Be Set Free (available at **http://worthypublishing.com/books/Idol-Lies/**)

ICE BREAKERS

(choose A or B to share and then go around the group to answer C)

A. Jonathan Edwards says we do what we most want to do. What does this tell you about your dominant desires?
B. What things do you think about the most? What does this tell you about your dominant desires?
C. What stood out to you from the video and why?

Tim Keller has a free sermon entitled "Removing Idols of the Heart" available at www.redeemer.com that would be so helpful for you to listen to on your own this week.

————

Prepare your heart for homework each day with prayer and music.

————

PERSONAL PRAYER: Pray through 1 Peter 4:1–2 this week. You could pray something like this: "Lord, put steel in my heart to say no to my idol, the way Christ said no to temptation. May I look to things above and to being set free. Make my dominant desire living for Your will."

SONG: "In Christ Alone" by Keith and Kristyn Getty.

————

DAY 1:
DOMINANT DESIRES

1. Read the third chapter, highlighting as you go.
    A. Choose two points to comment on. What are they and why did you choose them?

    B. A. W. Tozer said that the reason some people "find" God in ways that other believers do not has to do with their dominant desire. This goes along with what Jesus said is the most important commandment. What is that commandment, according to Matthew 22:37?

DAY 2:
THE POWER OF THE GOSPEL

Every world religion offers a philosophy and commands its followers to obey. Christianity is unique in that it offers a power that helps us obey. So often we trust this power for initial salvation, but then we work really hard in our own strength to live the Christian life. Instead, we need to also trust this power to equip us to walk by faith moment by moment, to turn from our idols and toward the living God.

2. Read Romans 1:16–17.

A. Why did Paul refuse to be ashamed of the gospel (verse 16)?

B. Look at page 49 in this book for Jack Miller's definition of the gospel. What are the two parts of the gospel?

C. Leslie gave an illustration from her life on page 49 and applied the gospel to help her achieve victory. What was the situation and how did each part of the gospel play a part in her repentance and faith?

3. Review Rebecca's story from pages 43–45 and explain the following:
    A. What problem was she trying to solve with food?

    B. What lie had she embraced and how did this show the deceitfulness of her heart?

    C. When she was afraid to let go of her idol, how did the second part of the gospel help her?

4. Now take a look at a visible sin in your life, then identify the invisible idol, and see how the gospel could help you.
    A. What lie are you believing when this idol tempts you?

B. Though there will be pain in turning from an idol (and it will fight), what do you know about Christ that would help you win?

C. Write out words for your soul here so you are ready for the next time you are tempted.

DAY 3:
SUPPRESSING THE TRUTH

5. Read Romans 1:18–25. This passage refers to outward idolatry, the making of images, which was common in biblical days. But soul idolatry is just as despicable, so this passage is just as relevant to us.
   A. What is the very first step in the downward spiral of sin, according to verse 18?

   B. How, according to verses 19–20, can God's glory be seen everywhere by everyone? (For more help see the opening to Psalm 19.)

   C. What is key, according to verse 21, in preventing this downward spiral?

   D. Take a moment right now to give glory and thanks to God for who He is and how He has blessed you in the last twenty-four hours.

DAY 4:
EXCHANGING THE TRUTH FOR A LIE

Whenever we give in to our idols, we have exchanged the truth for a lie. The illustration given in this passage is the practice of homosexuality, but we are naive if we think this passage could not have also been illustrated with a multitude of other sins, including the one that besets us.

6. Read Romans 1:24–27.

   A. What illustration did Paul give in verses 26–27 of exchanging the truth of God for a lie?

   B. What did you learn from Wesley Hill's testimony on pages 47–48?

   C. Though your temptation may be different from Wesley Hill's, when you are tempted, the lie may be the same: If you do not do this, you will have a "lesser life." What is, indeed, the truth?

7. Read Romans 1:28–32.

   A. When we are not willing to suffer to resist temptation, we are sucked into the downward spiral. Describe what happens to our mind and heart, according to verses 28–31.

B. Give an example from your own life to illustrate verse 32—how you sometimes not only practice a sin, you approve of others who practice it.

DAY 5:
HE WHO SUFFERS IS DONE WITH SIN

Understanding the lie behind his temptation to embrace a gay life-style—that not to do so would lead to a "lesser life"—was pivotal for Wesley Hill. The same principle is true for us whether we are resisting unforgiveness, gluttony, manipulation, or another sin. We will suffer at first as we endure through the temptation, but then comes the "Greater Life." We will experience intimacy with God and a joy and a strength that those who refuse to suffer will never know.

That is the truth we must receive in place of the lie. We will not be completely done with sin until, like Christ, we die and are resurrected. But we can experience the diminishing power of sin and increasing joy on this earth as we die to ourselves.

8. Read 1 Peter 4:1–2. What promise is there for the believer who is willing to suffer in order to say no to sin?

9. Read 2 Corinthians 4:16–18.
    A. Resisting temptation involves temporary suffering. What does this passage teach you that could help you not to lose heart?

B. What is the lie you tend to believe in a temptation you often face? Write down the truth you will put in its place.

10. Your success as this study continues depends on your dominant desire. What would you say is your dominant desire right now?

GROUP PRAYER: Each individual says a prayer about the specific truth that can take the place of a lie she believes. Let one or two others support her prayer. When there is a pause, the next individual lifts up her request.

LESSON 4:
A SHOCKING METAPHOR

This lesson is longer than the others and your facilitator may choose to do it over two weeks or skip some sections in discussion. (If you divide this into two weeks, go through question 12 the first week.)

VIDEO 4: A Shocking Metaphor (available at **http://worthy publishing.com/books/Idol-Lies/**)

ICE BREAKERS

A. Why do you think adultery leads to such intense emotional pain? Why do you think God calls it "treacherous" and "violent?" (God thunders at those who have betrayed their spouses. In Malachi 2:16, He condemns the unfaithful man, saying he "does violence to the one he should protect" [NIV].)

B. What stood out to you from the video and why?

_____

Prepare your heart daily with prayer and song.

_____

PERSONAL PRAYER: The consequences of running after our idols may feel severe, but God's purposes are always for our good. Pray through Hosea 2:14–15.

SONG: Consider singing "Jesus, Lover of My Soul" by Charles Wesley or "Arise, My Love" by Michael Card.

A free sermon you may wish to listen to on your own to help you understand how heart idols are like false lovers that hurt us is Tim Keller's "Christ, Our Life," available at Redeemer.com.

_____

DAY 1:
A METAPHOR TO AWAKEN US

According to rabbinic tradition, a kiss from God is a living word of prophecy. When a verse leaps out at you and speaks to your heart, you are being kissed by God—slow down, savor it, and contemplate what He is telling you.

1. Read the fourth chapter, highlighting as you go.
   A. Choose two points to comment on. What are they and why did you choose them?

B. Chapter 4 opens with a quote from Derek Kidner
(see page 55). According to Kidner, what can the
sexual metaphor help us understand about our relationship with God? How does it help you?

DAY 2:
HOSEA, THE BROKEN-
HEARTED BRIDEGROOM

The book of Hosea is God's expansive mural of a broken-hearted
bridegroom loving an unfaithful bride.

2. What did God ask of this prophet in Hosea 1:2 and why?

3. Hosea's wife, Gomer, had three children, and only the first
    was Hosea's. Then she returned to her lovers. Read Hosea
    2:5–8.
    A. In verse 5, what reason did Gomer give for return-
       ing to her lovers?

    B. In verses 6–7, how did the Lord respond to her and
       why?

    C. How did the Lord know how Gomer would
       respond (Hosea 2:7b)? What do you think of her
       response?

D. What did she not realize according to verse 8?

E. How have you been like Gomer in the past? How are you like Gomer today?

4. Read Hosea 2:9–13.
   A. What phrases stand out to you in this passage?

   B. Describe the Lord's emotion in Hosea 2:13.

5. Read Hosea 2:14–15.
   A. Where was God going to lead Gomer and what was He going to do there?

   B. What is His ultimate purpose, according to verse 15, for leading us into the wilderness?

   C. Be still before God and ask Him, "How does this relate to my life right now?" Is there a way God is speaking tenderly to you in whatever pain you are facing?

6. Read Hosea 2:16–23.
   A. How will God's people one day relate to Him (verse 16) and why (verse 17)?

B. In verse 18, God referred to the covenant, and in verses 19–20, He painted the covenant in terms of a marriage ceremony. What did God say He will do in this passage?

The phrase to know *in verse 20 is the intimate expression of marriage. As our hearts are transformed, as we find God to be our all in all, we will, indeed, experience an intimacy akin to the best that earthly marriage can offer.*

C. How will God one day reverse the names of Gomer's children according to verse 23?

This renewing of the covenant, this exchange between God and man ("You are My people!" "You are my God!") is repeated twice in the New Testament and can be helpful as you worship. As you study the scripture, let God quicken you, let Him call you, let Him make a verse radioactive to you. ("You are My people!") Then, in response, slow down, pray the verse, live it out. ("You are my God!")

7. Describe the scene in Hosea 3:1–3. Who won the bid at the auction? What does this say about God?

8. Why is it that you cannot experience the presence of the Lord while you are engaged with your idols? What does that mean to you today?

DAY 3:
AS A BRIDEGROOM REJOICES
OVER HIS BRIDE

The sexual metaphor has a positive aspect as well, one that should warm our hearts and give us confidence in our Bridegroom's commitment to us and His desire for intimacy with us. The best of earthly marriages, the most intimate moments that make us weep with love, are only a taste of what is to come with Christ. The Lord says this is a profound mystery (Ephesians 5:32).

9. What parallel did God make in Isaiah 62:5b? Try to put yourself in a bridegroom's place and describe what his feelings might be.

10. Turn back to Isaiah 1:18 and explain how the gospel makes it possible for Christ to completely delight in you.

11. In Zephaniah 3:17, find five descriptions of God's love for you.

In the poetic section of the Old Testament, we find two contrasting books side by side. The first, Ecclesiastes, has been called "the saddest song" because it shows a believer looking for love "under the sun," failing to realize God's love for him. In sharp distinction, the second, the Song of Songs, has been called "the sweetest song." Above all the biblical books, Charles Spurgeon says, it is the Song of Songs that shows us God's heart for us.

12. Read the Song of Songs 1:1–4. (Sometimes it is confusing to determine who is speaking in this poetic play. In the opening seven verses, though it varies between the individual bride and the corporate picture of the bride, it is always the "bride.")

   A. What did the bride want according to verse 2?

   B. How did she describe his love and then his name (verses 2–3)?

   C. Describe her longing (verse 4). Do you identify with this?

13. Read the Song of Songs 2:8–13.

   A. Describe what images come to mind as you read.

   B. What refrain is repeated in this passage? What do you think God is telling you through this?

The Song closes it as it began, with the longing of the bride, though it is a longing that has matured through trial. In the beginning (such as in 1:2), the Hebrew word for love is dowd, *referring to passion. Then He asks more of the Bride (such as in 2:13), using the Hebrew word* rayah, *meaning "committed love." By the close of the book, the Hebrew word for love is a combination of the two, meaning* ahabah *or "passionate, committed love." This is the covenant love God has for us, and which He longs for in return. You can see this love in 8:6–7.*

14. Read the Song of Songs 8:5–7.

    A. Describe the scene in 8:5a. What do you see in this?

    B. In what ways have "wilderness times" drawn you closer to the Lord?

    C. How is God's love described in verses 6–7? What does this mean to you?

15. Were you "kissed" by God during this lesson? If so, share.

DAY 4:
DO YOU FIND GOD USEFUL OR BEAUTIFUL?

With earthly love, often what you experience at first is not so much love, but what Lauren Winner calls "ego-blast." You are excited that someone so great is into you! But until you come to appreciate *his* beauty, it isn't really love, it's using someone for your own selfish gain.

In the same way, in our relationship with the Lord, we first long for what He can give us—salvation from hell, relief from suffering, material provisions . . . We may realize, as Gomer did in the book of Hosea and the younger son did in the story of the prodigal son, that it is better to be with Him than away from Him. But is that yet true love?

Jonathan Edwards reflected that religious people find God useful, but Christians find God beautiful. The Song of Songs is a poetic play in which the bride learns to find the bridegroom beautiful. The book is filled with mutual adoration. That is how our relationship with the Lord is meant to be.

Ezekiel 16 is a poetic play in which the bride finds her bridegroom useful. He adored her, but she used Him, taking everything He gives her and giving it to her idols. Historically, Israel formed alliances with other nations and participated in pagan idol worship. One frightening aspect of idolatry is that idols demand propitiation. They will take something precious from us: our health, our contentment, our children . . .

Ezekiel 16 is a miniature version of the book of Hosea. We will divide it into four "acts."

16. Read Ezekiel 16:1–14 (Act 1: God Bestows Grace and Beauty).
   A. Describe the state of the baby girl in verses 1–5.

   B. Describe God's response to her in verses 6–7.

   C. In verses 8–14, we see pictures of covenant love and how it can make us beautiful. Describe those images.

17. Read Ezekiel 16:15–22 (Act 2: The Unfaithful Bride).
   A. According to verse 15, what did the bride trust in, what did she become, and what did she do?

   B. According to verses 16–21, what did she do with each of the gifts God had given to her?

C. Though this passage speaks about a different culture with different "gods," we must not miss the parallel to our lives and our tendency to take God's gifts and use them to worship our idols. Think about the talents or spiritual gifts, the blessings of children, or material provisions God has given you. How might you take these and use them to increase your own reputation, comfort, or power instead of using them to glorify Him and to sacrifice for "the least of these"?

D. What was the bride's fatal mistake that led to her downward spiral (verse 22)?

18. How has God spoken to you through these first two "acts" in Ezekiel 16?

DAY 5:
A PROFOUND MYSTERY

Ezekiel 16 continues with the idols themselves turning on the bride and God allowing it to happen. This is His just wrath poured out upon His unfaithful bride, bringing us to the paradox of Scripture. God says He must punish sin, and yet, He so loves His bride. You hear His anguish in Hosea 11 when He remembered how when "Israel was a child," He loved him; how He "taught Ephraim how to walk;" how He "bent down to feed" him. In anguish He cried, "How can I give you up, O Ephraim?"

God's holiness demands that He must punish sin—and yet, how can He completely forsake us? He cannot. So He covenants that He will take the punishment on Himself, bearing what we deserve.

At the close of Ephesians, after Paul has described how earthly marriage should be mutual sacrifice and adoration, he says: "This mystery is profound, and I am saying that it refers to Christ and the church" (Ephesians 5:32). Whenever the New Testament talks about "the mystery," it is referring to the gospel. This mystery is hidden in Hosea and in Ezekiel 16, but we can see it better than they could, for we are on the other side of the cross.

19. Read Ezekiel 16:39–42 (an excerpt from Act 3: The Wrath of God).
    A. Describe the wrath of God that fell on His people. (This describes how Jerusalem fell.)

    B. We think our idols will help us, but then they turn and "cut us to pieces." They demand a payment to be appeased—they will take something precious from us. How have you experienced this?

20. Read Ezekiel 16:59–63 (an excerpt from Act 4: The Covenant).
    A. What does God say He will do concerning His faithless bride (verse 60)?

    B. What else stands out to you in this passage and why?

21. Read Ephesians 5:25–27.

    A. How, according to verse 25, did Christ love His
    bride, the Church?

    B. When you have doubts because life is hard or
    because God doesn't answer your prayers as you
    hoped, how can the above truth help you to be con-
    fident of His love for you?

    C. Find the reasons that Christ was motivated to die
    for us in verses 26 and 27.

*Paul used this image graphically when writing to the Corinthian church,
which was known for immorality and susceptibility to false teachers. He
said, "I feel a divine jealousy for you, since I betrothed you to one husband, to present you as a pure virgin to Christ" (2 Corinthians 11:2).
The truth of Christ's death for us should help us to remain pure, help us
not to doubt His love, help us to turn from false lovers and trust in Him.*

22. Think about times in the last twenty-four hours when
something bad came out of your mouth or life. What were
you trusting in rather than God? How might the gospel,
the fact of Christ's willingness to die for you, and the fact
of His power over death, help you to trust Him the next
time you face a similar situation?

23. What is your take-away for this week?

GROUP PRAYER: The group facilitator says the name of a person in the group. Two women pray for that person, then the facilitator says another woman's name and others pray for her until every member of the group is prayed for.

———

LESSON 5:
OUR CHEATING HEARTS

VIDEO 5: Our Cheating Hearts (available at **http://worthy publishing.com/books/Idol-Lies/**)

ICE BREAKERS

A. There is always pain involved in turning away from an idol. Those who are willing to suffer that pain do so because they believe God will eventually meet them. Have you experienced the pain or any of the fulfillment of the promise of God meeting you? If so, share.

B. What stood out to you from the video and why?

A free sermon that has been pivotal in setting many free is Tim Keller's message on Jeremiah 2 entitled "How Sin Makes Us Addicts." It is available at www.redeemer.com.

———

Prepare your heart daily with prayer and song.

———

PERSONAL PRAYER: The Lord uses many word pictures in Jeremiah 2 and more are listed in question 14. Find a new one each day and pray through it for yourself. For example, "Lord, may I not 'spread my legs' for false lovers, bringing shame to You and myself." "Lord, my idol has as strong a pull on me as the animal sex drive. Only You can deliver me, please change my heart."

SONG: Look up and sing "Purify My Heart" or "Create in Me a Clean Heart," or sing along with the YouTube version of Indelible Grace's "O Love That Will Not Let Me Go."

DAY 1:
LILY'S STORY

1. Read the fifth chapter, highlighting as you go.
    A. Choose two points to comment on. What are they and why did you choose them?

    B. What harm can fantasizing cause? How did it hurt Lily?

    C. Lily lamented, asking God, "Why can't I be happy like I was a year ago?" How did God respond and why did that help her?

DAY 2:
WHITHER THOU GOEST

2. Read Jeremiah 2:1–3.

   A. Describe what Israel was like at first, using the pictures God painted in verses 1 and 2.

   B. How, according to verse 3, did God feel about Israel and how did He protect her, as a groom protecting His bride?

   C. How do the above pictures make you feel? Explain.

3. Do you remember a "first love" time with the Lord when you were ready to follow Him anywhere? If so, describe what you remember about yourself and about your new "bridegroom."

4. Read Numbers 11:5–6.

   A. After their enthusiastic beginning, describe Israel's complaints. Why was this "selective memory"?

   B. The "wilderness" eventually reveals who loves God for Himself and who was following Him just for His blessings. What have wilderness times shown you about your own heart?

5. Read Jeremiah 2:4–5.

    A. What question does God ask in verse 5?

    B. How did the Israelites attempt to solve their unhappiness and what happened to them as a result (verse 5)?

    C. Give an example of facing discomfort, loneliness, or a difficult circumstance from your own daily life. Then specifically describe a foolish response and a wise response.

DAY 3:
SIN IS NOT BREAKING A RULE, IT'S BREAKING A HEART

6. Read Jeremiah 2:6 and describe some of the mercies Israel forgot.

7. Have you ever had the experience of loving someone lavishly, and yet they have forgotten that love? How did it make you feel?

In Exodus, the Israelites were delivered from the wrath of God when the blood of a lamb was placed on their doorposts. That exodus foreshadowed a much deeper exodus from slavery and of the blood of the Lamb of God. It is this lavish mercy, above all others, that we must remember whenever we face temptation.

DAY 4:
AN ATTRACTION AS STRONG AS AN ANIMAL SEX DRIVE

The Lord is trying to break through the denial of His children. We are so blind to our sin, so ready to deceive ourselves. But unless we see our sin, we have no hope. In this passage we repeatedly see the language of intervention.

8. Read Jeremiah 2:19–24.

    A. Denial is a real phenomenon. We believe lies so we can pursue our idols. Give examples of a few lies that deceive people (racists, alcoholics, gluttons, gossips, fornicators, coveters . . .) into pursuing idols.

    B. How, in verse 19, did God try to shake Israel awake to the consequences of idolatry?

    C. Then God gave a series of illustrations to try to tap in to their hearts. Find those in verses 20–24, describing the last one in detail.

9. Ask the Lord to shine His light into the darkness of your soul and reveal any lie you are telling yourself so that you can pursue your idol. Then tell yourself the truth.

10. Read Jeremiah 2:25.
    A. The Israelites were no longer in denial. They admitted they loved their idols. But how did they feel?

    B. Have you ever felt that way?

    C. The gospel shows us how loved we are. Imagine the enemy is telling you that God will not be there for you if you resist temptation. Speak the truth to your soul, using the evidence of the cross.

DAY 5:
THE FALSE LOVERS AND THE TRUE LOVER

One of the most frightening truths about idols is that they demand a propitiation, a price to appease them. If you give yourself over to power, you may lose your children; if you give yourself over to comfort, you may lose your health; if you give yourself over to approval, you may lose years of contentment.

11. Read Jeremiah 3:23–24.
    A. According to verse 24, what will our idols devour?

    B. What have your idols devoured in your life?

12. What must we do according to Jeremiah 3:25–4:4? What does this mean?

13. Our true Lover, instead of cutting us to pieces, allowed Himself to be cut to pieces. He paid the propitiation price Himself. Read Jeremiah 31:31–33 and describe the day that God described to Jeremiah.

We live in that day! The propitiation has been paid by our True Lover and He has given us His Spirit. Why would we run to false lovers? Bernard of Clairvaux calls God "a shy lover." When we are in the arms of another, He will not come to us. Repeatedly God articulates this truth with word pictures.

14. Find the picture in each of the following and explain what is being communicated:
    A. 2 Corinthians 11:2

    B. Psalm 45:10–11

    C. Song of Songs 2:13–16

15. There is no better place to be than in the arms of God. Are you beginning to experience more of His quiet presence as you turn from your idols? If so, share something about it.

16. What is your take-away this week and why?

GROUP PRAYER: Lift up sentences of thanksgiving and praise for what you are learning, how you are being set free, and for God's tender mercies.

LESSON 6:
WHEN THE EARTH SHAKES

VIDEO 6: When The Earth Shakes (available at **http://worthy publishing.com/books/Idol-Lies/**)

ICE BREAKERS

A. In a sentence, share a time in your life when suffering made no sense, but now, in retrospect, it makes some sense.

B. What stood out to you from the video and why?

Prepare your heart daily with prayer and song.

PERSONAL PRAYER: God gives us psalms of lament for our times of suffering—psalms that show us how to pray when we are at our lowest. Most of them begin with an honest expression of despair. At some point, usually, the Spirit reminds the psalmist of the character of God, and then the psalmist can express trust even if circumstances continue. Try praying through Psalm 13.

SONG: Possible songs include Katharina von Schlegel's "Be Still, My Soul" or Matt Redman's "Blessed Be Your Name."

DAY 1:
THE MYSTERY OF SUFFERING

1. Read the sixth chapter, highlighting as you go.

   A. Choose two points to comment on. What are they and why did you choose them?

   B. Take one illustration from this chapter. What does it teach you about the mystery of suffering, our limitations, and God?

DAY 2:
A SEVERE MERCY

It never seems like mercy when you are in the midst of suffering, and yet both Scripture and life confirm that God refines His body, His bride, through suffering. His purpose is not only for individual refining but also for the refining of the whole body. When our world is shaken, it reveals the futility of our idols and the only One who can be our solid rock. God has all eternity in view, and too often we have only this earthly life in view.

2. Read Jeremiah 2:26–28.

   A. According to verses 26–27, how did the kings, officials, priests, and prophets regard their idols?

   B. How did their idols fail them, according to verse 28?

3. Read Acts 4:32 through Acts 5:11.

   A. What beauty do you see in the early church as described in Acts 4:32–37?

   B. What ugliness do you see in the lives of Ananias and Sapphira? What do you think might have been their deep idols leading to the visible sin?

   C. What happened to Ananias and then to Sapphira? Why, do you think?

   D. How well did their idols help them in their day of trouble? How does this apply to your soul idols?

   E. How did this event, according to verses 5 and 11, impact the early church?

4. How we respond to suffering reveals where our trust lies. If we continue to trust in our idols, we will dig in our heels. If we turn, instead, to God, we will be changed. Read Jeremiah 2:29–32 and find phrases that show how God's people responded in Jeremiah's day to His shaking of their worlds.

DAY 3:
THE GREAT I AM

God will not only make His disobedient children examples to the Church, He will refine His most extraordinary vessels. When you consider the people He used mightily, you realize that each suffered tremendously. We know, for example, that He loved Mary, Martha, and Lazarus—yet He took them through the fire.

5. In the book, how did Ed and Cynthia respond to the shaking of their worlds (pages 96–98)?

6. How are you responding, right now, to any shaking going on in your life?

7. What did you learn about Jesus as the I AM on pages 101–104? Was anything new to you? If so, explain.

8. Read John 11:1–16 and find evidences that Jesus loved Lazarus yet chose not to come running.

The Greek word translated stayed *has the connotation of endured. There are times the Lord endures our suffering because He has a greater plan for us or for His corporate body.*

9. Jesus gently chastised Martha in Luke 10 because He knew her idol was causing her pain and that she needed to

trust Him instead. Here we go again. Read John 11:17–28
carefully.

A. What did Martha do and say in verses 20–21? Do
   you see any control or manipulation behind her
   words? Explain your answer.

B. What did Martha think that Jesus meant, according
   to her response to Him in verse 24?

C. What did Jesus claim in verse 25?

D. Jesus referred to Himself by the name God spoke
   to Moses (I AM who I AM). In all of the great I AMs
   in John, the friends of Jesus were in awe, and His
   enemies wanted to stone him. (See John 11:53.)
   Why did His words provoke such strong reactions?

E. What question did Jesus ask Martha in verse 26 and
   how did she respond in verse 27?

*I believe this was when Martha's control idol cracked. Her idol had not
been able to help her in her "day of trouble," but the great I AM could,
and she surrendered. Then she went to get Mary—before she was pulling
Mary away from Jesus, now she was sending her to Him.*

DAY 4:
JESUS WEPT

10. Read John 11:29–44.

    A. Mary and Martha spoke exactly the same words to Jesus. Why do you think He responded so differently to them?

    B. Find phrases in the above passage that show the various emotions Jesus felt because of the death of Lazarus.

    C. Jesus could have stopped Lazarus' death and did not, for He had higher goals than delivering His beloved from temporary suffering. What might have been some of those goals?

11. Does it help alleviate your suffering to know God cares for you? Why or why not?

DAY 5:
WHEN THE EARTH SHOOK

We can know that suffering for a believer is never punishment, for Jesus took that punishment on the cross.

12. Read Matthew 27:50–54.

A. Describe what happened on earth when Jesus died.

B. Why, do you think?

C. What was the reaction of the centurion and those who were with him?

D. What does this mean to you when your life is shaken?

13. Read Hebrews 12:25–29.
    A. What warning are we given in verse 25?

    B. What promise and meaning do you find in verses 26–27?

    C. What, according to verses 28–29, should we remember in the midst of suffering? How should those truths cause us to respond?

14. What is your take-away this week and why?

GROUP PRAYER: The facilitator should lift up each woman's name and two others should pray for her until everyone in the group has received prayer. If your group is large, divide into smaller groups.

LESSON 7:
WHY WE CAN'T JUST SAY NO

This week we will look at passages from Romans 6, 7, and 8—key passages for transformation. This is a practical week during which you prepare your battle plan. I encourage you to use a modern Bible translation such as J. B. Phillips, the New Living Translation, or *The Message* if possible. (As one woman told me, "Romans 6, 7, and 8 make my head hurt, but *The Message* helps!")

VIDEO 7: Why We Can't Just Say No (available at **http://worthy publishing.com/books/Idol-Lies/**)

ICE BREAKERS

A. What is something you know you should not do, yet you still have a tendency to do it? (Or that you should do, yet you do not do?)
B. What stood out to you from the video and why?

Prepare your heart daily with prayer and song.

PERSONAL PRAYER: Pray through Romans 6:13 or any verse in these chapters that quickens you.

SONG: Possibilities include Robert Lowry's "Nothing but the Blood" and Casting Crowns' version of "Who Am I?"

———————

DAY 1:
THE SIN WITHIN

1. Read the seventh chapter, highlighting as you go.
   A. Choose two points to comment on. What are they and why did you choose them?

   B. Meditate on Romans 7:8 from *The Message* on pages 109–110. What does it say? Have you experienced this? Explain.

DAY 2:
FOLLOWING CHRIST OR
IDENTIFYING WITH HIM

When we try to *follow* Christ, we will fail. But if we *identify* with Him, we will find power. Dr. David Needham illustrates this with a common scenario: A new television program comes on and you are immediately aware this is something that will incite your particular lusts, rooted in your idols, whatever those may be. One approach is to tell yourself, *I shouldn't watch this. I should turn this off.* You are a "house divided" and your old nature may win or feel profoundly disappointed and keep longing to return. But instead of just "saying no," Needham suggests this approach:

For a moment you find yourself saying, "I want to watch this even though I know I shouldn't." Then, with a sudden jolt, the gracious Holy Spirit reminds you of something so very important. "Hey, wait a minute!" you say. "Who am I anyway? Is watching this stuff truly compatible with who I really am. . . . Life for me is not . . . fantasy vacations, a perfect figure, an envious reputation. . . . I know who I am—I am fundamentally a spiritual being created by God to display Jesus. Life—real life—is right there."

So I walk to the TV set and turn it off. No last, longing look this time.

Needham is right—who we *really* are will one day be manifest when all the dross is burned away and the gold is left. This is Christ in us, our hope of glory. Your idols and the rotten fruit they produce are not who you really are. They stand in the way of becoming who you really are. They are not your life. Christ is your life.

2. Paul used the picture of baptism in Romans 6:3–5—of going under the water and rising again—to illustrate saying good-bye to one life, leaving it under water, and saying hello to a new life.

   A. What question is in Romans 6:1, and how is it answered?

   B. What other question is asked in Romans 6:2? How is this phrased in *The Message*?

We get our identity, not from others, and not even from ourselves, but from God. Becoming a Christian means you not only start to follow Christ but you also identify with Him; you become part of Him.

213

3. Read Romans 6:5–11.

    A. What is the summary of this paragraph (verse 11)? What is the negative (to whom do you no longer belong?) and what is the positive (who are you?)?

    B. Take a common temptation such as gossip or stinginess and show how Romans 6:11, as illustrated by Needham's approach, could lead to victory. Be specific—this is practice!

A story is told of St. Augustine, who left his sexually promiscuous lifestyle. When he was approached by a former lover who said, "Augustine—Augustine—it's me!" he said, "I know. But it's not me." He was a new man in Christ.

DAY 3:

THEREFORE PRESENT YOURSELF NOT TO YOUR OLD MASTER BUT TO YOUR NEW

Overcoming sin is synergistic. We do not just passively expect God to deliver us, but we respond to His Spirit. Larry Crabb uses the term "dependent responsibility."

Romans 6:12–14 fleshes out how this works: Since we no longer belong to sin, but to Christ, we must present our members (our minds, our tongues, our hands . . .) not to sin but to Christ. The victory begins internally, with a mental choice to turn from the idol and toward God. It always involves faith that God will be to you what your idol can never be. All this is invisible. But it will flesh itself out visibly as you present your "members" to God. For example, instead of using your tongue to criticize or manipulate, the tongue will be used to pray or to encourage. Instead of using your hand to write a check for an expensive new toy, you write one for helping the helpless. Instead of using your eyes for unedifying books and blogs, you will use your eyes for edifying books and blogs.

4. Read Romans 6:12–14 carefully.

    A. We were born spiritually dead and in bondage, but that is not who we are anymore. Find two negative commands in verses 12 and 13a.

    B. Now, because we are spiritually alive, set free, and belong to Christ, what two positive commands can you find in verse 13?

    C. We do not have to sin, for God provides a way of escape when we obey Him. Take a temptation common to you (a besetting sin) and explain how you would:

        1) Internally, talk to your soul about who you really are and why God can be trusted to be to you what your idol can never be.

        2) Externally, how would this flesh itself out? What would you turn away from and what would you put in its place?

5. In Romans 6:15–19 Paul uses an illustration of slavery. What does he say?

6. Each time you identify with Christ to say no to the flesh, you become stronger. Is there a way you have experienced this? If so, share.

DAY 4:
THE LAW IS GOOD, BUT IT IS INSUFFICIENT TO CHANGE US

Romans 7 shows why we can't "just say no." Paul opens with a challenging analogy to marriage, saying that we are no longer "married" to the law, for God now has given us His Spirit. As promised in Hosea and in other prophets, there is a new power, and we must walk in that power, rather than trying to obey the law by ourselves.

7. Read Romans 7:7–11.
   A. Why is the law good, according to verse 7?

   B. How does sin pervert the law, according to verses 8 and 11?

   C. Dee's father commanded her not to ride her bike down a hill. That command became a temptation to her. Give an example from your life on how you have perverted a command into a temptation.

8. Using Romans 7:14–20, explain why we cannot obey the law in our own strength.

9. What is the answer, according to Romans 7:24–25?

10. What truth is given in Romans 8:1?

In every other religion, you work to gain a god's approval. In Christianity, because of Jesus, you are approved of. Then, out of love, you serve Him gratefully. This understanding is crucial in living the gospel-transformed life.

For example, I now am aware of how often I have manipulative or controlling thoughts concerning what I could say or do to try to "fix" people. Sin still dwells in me. But I see it now, because God has shown me my depravity. The gospel sheds light into my dark soul and my control idol. I see the lie. I am not better than others—I am so bad Christ had to die for me! But I also know Christ went all the way to the cross for me and for them. Because of this, I can also trust Him to fix the people that need fixing. If He wants me to be part of that, He will lead me to pray, to speak the truth in love, or to be silent. I must give control to Him.

11. Take the above illustration and explain how it depends on gospel truth to:
    A. Repent.

    B. Walk in faith.

    C. Where are you still struggling? What lie are you believing and what truth could you speak to your soul based on the gospel?

DAY 5:
FEED THE NEW MAN,
STARVE THE OLD MAN

If Christ now lives within us, we truly do have a new nature that needs nurturing. He will grow stronger as we feed him, and our former self, the old man, will grow weaker as we starve him. Who are you, really? Who do you want to feed?

12. The word "gospel" means good news. Good news is something that has happened in the past and is being joyfully reported. Good advice is something that is suggested to do in the future. According to Romans 8:1–4, what has already happened?

13. Romans 8:4 reiterates what we must do if we know who we really are. What is it?

14. Read Romans 8:5–7.
    A. What negative and positive instructions are given concerning your mind?

    B. How could you obey this better than you are? Be specific and realistic.

15. What is happening in you if you belong to God, according to Romans 8:9–11?

16. Read Romans 8:12–17.

   A. Who are you according to this passage?

   B. Resisting our idols involves suffering, but there is also a promise in verse 17. Find it.

17. What is your take-away from this week and why?

GROUP PRAYER: You've heard where each person in your group is weak. Get in pairs or groups of three to pray for one another.

LESSON 8:
IDOLS CANNOT BE REMOVED, ONLY REPLACED

VIDEO 8: Idols Cannot Be Removed, Only Replaced (available at http://worthypublishing.com/books/Idol-Lies/)

ICE BREAKERS

A. Share something you pursued, whether a material object or a goal, that brought you some joy but also brought disappointment because it didn't do all you hoped it would.
B. What stood out to you from the video and why?

Prepare your heart daily with prayer and song.

PERSONAL PRAYER: Pray through the psalms suggestion in question 14.

SONG: Possible songs include "Come, Thou Fount of Every Blessing" in the traditional or contemporary version, "My Hope Is in You" by Aaron Shust, and "In Christ Alone" by Keith and Kristyn Getty.

DAY 1:
THE EXPULSIVE POWER OF A NEW AFFECTION

1. Read the eighth chapter, highlighting as you go.
   A. Choose two points to comment on. What are they and why did you choose them?

   B. How would you summarize the heart of this chapter? Which illustration most illuminated this for you?

DAY 2:
CREATED TO WORSHIP

(For those interested, Thomas Chalmers' essay "The Expulsive Power of a New Affection" is available online.)

2. Thomas Chalmers says "a sensitive being" suffers without an object of worship. Can you relate to this? If so, explain.

3. James Noriega put it like this: "We worshiped our way into this mess, and by God's grace, we will worship our way out."

   A. Give an example from your life (or if you cannot, then from this chapter) of "worshiping your way into a mess." Be specific.

   B. Give an example from your life (or if you cannot, then from this chapter) of "worshiping your way out." Be specific.

4. Read Ecclesiastes 2:1–11.

   A. Here is a man who had the power and money to get what many of us think will satisfy us, if we could only attain them. What were some of the ways "under the sun" (in other words, apart from God and eternity) he tried to satisfy his soul?

   B. Often during the pursuit of something other than God, we find excitement and pleasure (see verse 10), but at the end of that pursuit, we have different feelings. Describe them based on verse 11.

5. Read Philippians 3:8–9.

   A. What is Paul's testimony here?

B. How does he now see the things in which he once found his identity and value?

DAY 3:
THE GIRL NO ONE WANTED

6. Read Genesis 29:16–31.

    A. What contrasts do you find between Rachel and Leah in verses 16–18?

    B. What did Laban do in verses 19-23 and why?

    C. How did Jacob respond in verse 25, and how do you think Leah felt?

    D. How long did Leah have Jacob to herself?

    E. What are we told about Jacob in verse 30?

    F. Who did love Leah, according to verse 31, and how was that love shown?

7. Wanting a person's love is not a bad thing, but when it becomes an ultimate goal, like any idol, it will eventually

turn and hack us to pieces. Can you identify with this? If so, explain.

8. Read Genesis 29:31–35.
   A. What names did Leah give her first three sons and what did each mean?

   B. How did these names reflect her *epithumia* (overwhelming desire)?

   C. Idols demand a price. What did Leah give up during the years she worshiped her idol?

   D. What did she name her fourth son, what did it mean, and why do you think she changed?

Leah's turn from her idol to the one true God led to many blessings, though most she would not see until after her life on earth was over.

9. In that patriarchal culture, women were rarely valued or mentioned. Do your best to find ways that God met Leah, cared for Leah, and allowed her to have a lasting legacy through Judah, the son that marked her turn from idolatry.

A. Genesis 29:31

B. Genesis 30:17

C. Genesis 49:29–33 (Do you see any tenderness here for Leah in Jacob's dying words?)

D. Ruth 4:11

E. Hebrews 7:14

F. Revelation 5:5

10. Thomas Chalmers said that the desire for sin and the desire for God cannot exist at the same time in the human heart— one will always push out the other. How does Leah's story demonstrate the expulsive power of a new affection?

DAY 4:
THIS TIME I WILL PRAISE THE LORD

11. "Worship" comes from the same root word as "worth." Often we can tell what is of the greatest value to us by asking, "What, if we lost it, would make life not worth living?" Ask yourself this again. How would you answer?

12. On page 128, Dee lists some ordinary means of grace that helped her set her affections on Christ. What were they?

13. How might you incorporate any of the above into your life so that you can put on Christ?

14. Believers from Basil to Bonhoeffer to Bono have found that praying the psalms helps them to worship. Today, pray Psalm 27 a few verses at a time. Here's a sample prayer for the first, but make it your own.

    A. Psalm 27:1–3: *I do not need to be afraid of* _____ _____ *for You are my light and my salvation. No matter what comes against me, I can be confident because You are in control.*

    B. Psalm 27:4

    C. Psalm 27:5–6 (This says, "I will sing and make melody to the LORD." List a few songs you can easily sing throughout the day—and then do it!)

    D. Psalm 27:7–10

    E. Psalm 27:11–14

DAY 5:
LEARNING FROM RACHEL'S LIFE

15. Read Genesis 30.

    A. What did Rachel feel she had to have for life to have meaning? Why?

    B. Idolatry leads to distorted prayers, methods, and relationships. Find all of these in Rachel's life in Genesis 30:1–15.

    C. Children are a gift from God, yet when they become our life, we are likely to bring harm to them and to ourselves. What are some red flags for being too enmeshed with children?

In Genesis 31, Rachel stole her father's household gods when the family was fleeing Laban. Leslie Williams writes: "Without knowing fully what we are doing, we hide the things we secretly love and admire under our skirts, like Rachel, sitting primly and righteously on our camels, wondering why we are not whole, why we still suffer, why we feel unreconciled to the God we profess."

16. Meditate on the above quote from Leslie Williams and then answer the following:

    A. Describe some of the ways Rachel suffered as a result of her heart idols.

B. Williams says we hide the things we secretly love—we may hide our heart idols from others, but also from ourselves. How has this study opened your eyes to any secret idols?

C. What suffering has clinging to your idols brought into your life?

17. What is your take-away this week and why?

GROUP PRAYER: Gather in pairs or groups of three, confess where your souls are idolatrous, and pray for one another.

————

LESSON 9:
RESPONDING TO OUR ONE TRUE LOVER

VIDEO 9: Responding to Our One True Lover (available at **http://worthypublishing.com/books/Idol-Lies/**)

ICE BREAKERS

A. Every earthly love story that moves us taps in to the truer heavenly love story. Think of a book or movie with a love story that touched you. What parallel do you see between the male protagonist and Jesus?

B. What stood out to you from the video and why?

———

Prepare your heart daily with prayer and song.

———

PERSONAL PRAYER: Find a passage that is meaningful to you from the Song of Songs or Psalm 45 and pray through it.

SONG: "Jesus, Lover of My Soul" in the traditional or contemporary version, "I Will Follow" by Jason Ingram, Reuben Morgan, and Chris Tomlin, or "Jesus, I Come," a hymn written by William Sleeper and put to a contemporary melody for Indelible Grace by Greg Thompson, available on YouTube.

———

DAY 1:
ARISE, MY LOVE

In the opening of the Song of Songs, the bride was euphoric in her newfound rest in her bridegroom. But in the section we will study, she has drifted away. Hudson Taylor writes:

> Maybe the very restfulness of her newfound joy made her feel too secure. Maybe she thought that as far as she was concerned, there was no need for the exhortation, "Dear children, keep yourselves from idols" (1 John 5:21). . . . Maybe she hardly thought at all. Glad to be saved and free, she forgot the world's current course was against her.

In the Christian life, our Bridegroom continually challenges us to move higher with Him, dying more to ourselves, to our idols, and to what often feels "safe."

1. Read the Song of Songs 2:13–17.

    A. What did the bridegroom ask of his bride in verse 13?

    B. Where was she hiding, and what did he want, according to verse 14?

    C. Our fears can be just as detrimental to the fruit in our life as foxes are to grapevines. What fears have kept you from going higher with God?

    D. What did the bride tell the bridegroom to do in verse 17?

    E. How does Hudson Taylor interpret this passage? (See page 135.)

This passage is followed by a bad dream in which the bride cannot find her Bridegroom. Though we will never lose our relationship with Jesus, we can lose fellowship with Him, quenching His Spirit by refusing Him, sending Him away. But even the sense of His absence can work on our hearts, making us long for Him, making us desirous of hearkening to His call.

2. Are you becoming more aware of the sense of God's presence or His absence? If so, share.

3. Read Song of Songs 4:6–7 and explain how the bride responded when her bridegroom came for her again.

4. God is a God of second chances. Though you may have regrets about a way you responded in the past, you can use those regrets to respond rightly in another situation. Have you experienced this? If so, share.

DAY 2:
MESS WITH MY HEART, O GOD

In the book, Hope asks God to mess with her heart if she was wrong about opposing adoption, and He did, through the devotional *My Utmost for His Highest*. Read what she read from Chambers on page 135 of this book.

5. Does the quote from Oswald Chambers speak to you in any way, or not? Explain.

The Chambers devotional for that day was based on Jeremiah 4:1. We have already looked at Jeremiah 2 and 3, where God used the language of intervention, the shocking metaphor of an adulteress, and pleaded with His Bride because her idols had already taken so much from her.

6. For review and context, read Jeremiah 3:22–25.
   A. What plea did God make (verse 22) and what reason did He give (verse 23)?

B. What did the Israelites lose by clinging to idols and working at cross-purposes with God (verse 24)?

C. What response would be appropriate (verse 25)?

"O Israel," says the LORD,
"if you wanted to return to me, you could.
You could throw away your detestable idols
and stray away no more."
(Jeremiah 4:1, NLT)

7. Read the above and also the same verse in the translation you're using.
   A. Though the Israelites have told God "it is hopeless" (Jeremiah 2:25), He gave them hope. Find it.

   B. What must they do in order to find freedom?

   C. Our spiritual growth charts, once we have seen our idols, will still have dips, plateaus, and even plunges—but they should move steadily up. How have you seen growth in your life since beginning this study?

PERSONAL PRAYER EXERCISE: Is there an area where you feel you should dare to pray Hope's prayer ("Mess with my heart, O God")? If so, do it here, between you and God.

DAY 3:
RESPONDING TO HURT AS
CHRIST RESPONDED

The same heart idol can manifest itself in different ways. One of the ways Hope's control idol manifested itself was in a lack of forgiveness, especially toward her father. So often we want to "help" God discipline a person who has injured us by withholding complete forgiveness. For Hope, the light turned on when she realized that true forgiveness always demands a price. She was going to have to suffer, as Christ did, to give true grace.

8. What command and reason for the command do we find in Ephesians 4:32?

Moments before he died, Dietrich Bonhoeffer, who was martyred because he tried to stop Hitler, asked God to forgive those carrying out his hanging. He mirrored what Christ did and what so many martyrs have done. (See Acts 7:60.) Bonhoeffer said that true forgiveness always demands suffering.

9. Read Matthew 18:23–35.
   A. Summarize the parable and the main point.

   B. What do you think "forgiving from the heart" (verse 35) looks like?

C. What are some pseudo ways to "forgive" and why should we run from them?

10. Read 1 Peter 2:21–25.
    A. To what have we been called (verse 21)?

    B. How is it that Christ found strength when persecuted (verses 22–23)?

    C. Idols cannot be removed, only replaced. How could trust in God help you to let go of control and forgive from your heart?

11. How is the Lord speaking to you concerning forgiveness?

DAY 4:
THE IDOL OF "WORKS RIGHTEOUSNESS"

Hope had to stop trying to be the perfect Proverbs 31 wife. It's so subtle but it is easy to find our identity in being a good Christian instead of being in Christ. We go to church, give money, serve in ministry, train our children—not so much out of adoration of God but so that others will see us as good Christians or so that we can feel good about ourselves. Instead of resting in Christ and finding our identity in Him, we are trusting in how "righteous" we appear to ourselves and to others.

12. Read Philippians 3:1–10.

    A. Where could Paul have found his identity?

    B. How did he come to see that?

    C. Where did he find his identity instead and what was his goal?

    D. If you were to write a personal parallel of this passage, what might you write?

13. Read Habakkuk 3:17–19.

    A. God had told Habakkuk that a purging was coming, so Habakkuk was braced for the worst. How did he say he would respond if the labor of his hands failed?

    B. If you had to brace yourself for the worst in your life, do you think you could respond like Habakkuk? Why or why not?

    C. What did Madeleine L'Engle say about the "perfect family" and what she believes God has really called us to do (page 140)? Do you agree or not? Explain.

DAY 5:
HEAR, O DAUGHTER, CONSIDER, AND INCLINE YOUR EAR

As we grow in our understanding of God's love for us, we can let go of our idols, of our false identities, and rest in Him. One of the most beautiful passages about responding to our one true lover is Psalm 45. In many ways it is a condensed version of the Song of Songs.

14. Read Psalm 45:1–9 as a love poem. Write down the passages describing our returning King Jesus that most penetrate your heart, and explain why.

15. On the basis of who God is, what are we asked to do in Psalm 45:10? What do you think this means?

16. How is "the Bride" described in verses 13–15?

17. How can this passage help you to "put off" your idols and "put on" Christ?

18. What is your take-away this week and why?

GROUP PRAYER: Have one person lift up each woman's name while the others pray sentence prayers for her. If your group is large, divide into smaller groups for this prayer.

LESSON 10:
WHAT ANGELS LONG TO SEE

VIDEO 10: What Angels Long to See (available at **http://worthy publishing.com/books/Idol-Lies/**)

ICE BREAKERS

A. Name a way that you are beginning to understand how the gospel can save you, not just from the penalty of sin, but also its power.

B. What stood out to you from the video and why?

———

Prepare your heart daily with prayer and song.

———

PERSONAL PRAYER: Pray through 1 Peter 1:10–13 for yourself, asking that you might better understand the breadth of God's love and power for you.

SONG: "Mighty to Save" by Rodney Clawson or "Rock of Ages," which was written in 1763 by Augustus Montague Toplady.

———

DAY 1:
HOW THE GOSPEL CAN RESCUE THE RICH AND THE POOR

1. Read the final chapter, highlighting as you go. Choose two points to comment on.

2. Read Proverbs 30:8–9.
   A. Why did Agur ask God not to give him riches? Would you ever pray that way?

   B. Why did Agur ask to be spared poverty? Can you identify?

Review this definition of the gospel:
> We are more sinful than we could ever imagine (for Christ had to die).
> We are more loved than we ever dared dream (for He *did* die).

3. Read James 1:9–10. How does this passage show how the gospel could rescue the lowly brother (the poor) but also the rich brother?

DAY 2:
IDOLS DELUDE AND DEMAND PROPITIATION

4. Read Zechariah 10:1–2.

   A. What power, according to verse 1, does God have and why?

   B. In contrast, find everything you can about what idols promise and actually do in verse 2.

5. Idols "promise consolation" but then turn on us. What price did Nicki's idol demand of her?

6. At the end of this story, Dee shares that Nicki was still living with her boyfriend. She says Nicki was "managing" her idol (page 158). What does that mean? Do you see that happening in your life? Explain.

In The Great Divorce, *C. S. Lewis tells of a character who kept a red lizard on his shoulder that the angel wanted to kill. That seemed too drastic a measure to the character, but the angel told him it was the only way to be free.*

7. Jesus said "You will know the truth, and the truth will set you free" (John 8:32). The Spirit of God had to keep bringing the truth to Dee. Consider how her One True Lover kept speaking to her, breaking through her delusion.

A. In the opening chapter, Dee shares that she first became aware of her control idol through the bad fruit it produced and through a sermon called "Models of Manipulation." What do you remember about that?

B. When Dee stood in front of her plundered jewelry box, she didn't want to forgive. How is that a manifestation of the control idol?

C. The Lord brought a scene from *Les Misérables* to her mind. How is this scene a picture of the gospel?

8. Share a few specific ways your One True Lover is breaking through the delusion of your idol.

DAY 3:
THE GOSPEL SHOWS US HOW NEEDY WE ARE AND HOW LOVED WE ARE

It is so easy to trust in religion instead of Christ, to look at how we are following the rules instead of seeing our great need and our great Rescuer. (Tim Keller's messages on the parable of the prodigal son are available in free sermons on Redeemer.com. Look for the messages on Luke 15.)

9. Read Luke 15:1–3.

    A. To whom is Jesus speaking? How do you know?

    B. How can you see that these scribes and Pharisees did not grasp the gospel (verse 2)?

    C. What then, were they trusting in? (See also Luke 18:9.)

    D. What price do religious idols demand of those who trust in them?

10. Read Luke 15:11–19.

    A. What evidence can you find for the younger son not loving his father for who his father was (verse 12–13)?

    B. What might have been the younger son's heart idol?

    C. How did that idol delude and what price did it extract from him (verses 14–16)?

    D. When he came to his senses, how did the younger son see his father differently (verse 17)?

E. What did he plan to say to his father (verse 19)?

F. How have you "come to your senses" during this journey? Be specific.

11. Read Luke 15:20–24.
   A. Find everything you can to describe the extravagant love of the father.

   B. In what ways does this reflect the gospel?

   C. True repentance always leads to a celebration! How have you experienced this in your life?

   D. How did this picture help Nicki begin to turn from her idol?

   E. How could this picture help you?

DAY 4:
THE SUBTLETY OF RELIGIOUS IDOLS

Both in the days of Jesus and today, it is common for a religious person or a Christian to think he is trusting in God when he is really trusting in his own righteousness. This was the delusion of the older brother and of the Pharisees to whom Jesus speaks. It can indeed hinder our own growth and intimacy with our True Lover.

12. Read Luke 15:25–32.
    A. When the older brother heard that his younger brother was home "safe and sound," how did he respond—and why, do you think?

    B. Look carefully at what he said to his father (verses 29 and 30) and find evidences for a "heart of stone" toward both his father and his brother.

    C. What was the older brother trusting in? How did that idol fail him?

    D. Describe the extravagant love of the father to the older brother.

13. Have you ever felt as if God let you down because you served Him or kept rules, yet He didn't give you what you wanted? If so, what was wrong about your thinking?

DAY 5:
THE BEAUTY AND POWER
OF THE GOSPEL

14. What has this study revealed to you about the darkness in your heart? Have you been able to see the idols, the beasts within? What has God shown you?

15. What has this study revealed to you about God's love for you? Have you been able to trust Him enough to let go of your idol and ask Him to come to you? Explain.

16. What do you think will be the lasting impact of this study on your life? Name three specifics.

GROUP PRAYER: Take turns giving praise to God for what He has done and is doing in your life.

Leader's Notes

Thank you for facilitating this study. Never have I seen truths so dramatically change lives—I anticipate you will see the same! Your role in prayer and encouragement is vital. Here are ways to make this group the best it can be.

EXPRESSING CHRIST'S LOVE

- During the week, pray for each woman by name. Pray for the group to be a welcoming and loving place.
- Greet each woman warmly each week and email or Facebook them during the week, letting them know they are valued.
- Make emails and phone numbers available for the group so they can bond with one another.
- Plan a special lunch or evening about halfway through the study and have the women share how they are being changed.
- Listen between the lines—sometimes you may feel led to visit a woman outside of study to express Christ's love to her.

PREPARING THE VIDEOS

- Each weekly session opens with a video. They are available for free at **http://worthypublishing.com/books/Idol-Lies/**. They are ten to twenty minutes each and include teaching from Dee and testimonies from other women. You'll probably want to download them on a computer ahead of time so they are ready when you want to show them. After downloading them, you can connect your computer to a large screen for a large group or simply show them on a small screen if your group is at a small table. Here are instructions for doing this—it's not hard, but a young techie person could help you if you have never done this!

- David Powlison has four video clips under three minutes each on idolatry that are very illuminating. You might want to play one a week for weeks 2 through 6. You can find them all at http://www.ccef.org/video/keeping-ourselves-idol-worship
- Consider showing an hour video on idolatry from Tim Keller sometime—perhaps a special evening, or you could hand out books the first session, get acquainted, and watch it then. It is called "The Grand Demythologizer" (available at www.thegospelcoalition.com and other websites).

ENCOURAGING HOMEWORK

- Encourage members to do their homework for their own growth and to be a good friend in the group. If they do this, they not only enrich the discussion, but you can skip the information-gathering questions (listed by chapter below). If the group tends to neglect the homework, call a few of the more mature women privately and ask them to be models for the others. You could also pair up accountability partners and put a more mature woman with a less mature one.
- Group attendance tends to average two-thirds, so a maximum group membership size should be twelve (so eight are usually present) for optimum sharing and pace. (Larger groups can begin together with video and video questions and then divide into smaller discussion groups.)
- If you opt to divide the lessons and do them in twenty sessions, watch the video and do two days the first half, and finish the last three days in the last half. Some groups find it hard to get through lesson 4 in just one week because the women have so

much to say. So you may want to plan to divide that even if you are not dividing the other lessons.

KEEPING THE DISCUSSION STRONG

- Think of yourself as a facilitator that keeps the ball going to everyone instead of a volley between you and the group. Accomplish that by keeping these things in mind:
  - Occasionally go around the group asking everyone the same question.
  - Ask, "What does someone else think?"
  - If a woman in the group tends to monopolize the conversation, pray for her and, if necessary, speak gently and privately to her, asking her to help you draw the others out.
  - Watch for facial expressions. If a quiet woman seems almost ready to speak, gently ask her, "Did you have a thought?"
  - Avoid tangents, and keep the group moving.

YOUR FIRST MEETING

Do Lesson 1 unless the group members are just receiving their books today and have not been able to do homework. In that case, have a get-acquainted time and watch "The Grand Demythologizer" video together. (See pages 245–246 about preparing the videos.) Then ask each woman to share what stood out to her from the video.

LESSON 1: LAYERS OF LIES

- Always watch the video first, then gather in as small a circle as possible and hear from as many as possible on the Ice Breakers.

- Information-gathering questions that could be skipped in discussion: 2a, 5, 8.
- *Q1d*: Give special emphasis to this question.
- *Q6*: If no one shares on this one, you may need to vulnerably lead the way.
- *Q9*: This is an important exercise, be sure to give enough time.
- *Q10*: For example, wanting human approval more than God's could lead to coveting, stealing, and slandering.
- *Q11*: Loving God—and idols keep you from intimacy with God.
- *Q17*: Idols must be replaced, so seeing the deep heart idol could signal to Martha that she is not trusting God and could help her move not only away from her sin but toward God.

LESSON 2: SPIRITUAL BLINDNESS

- Information-gathering questions that could be skipped in discussion: 2a, 8a, 8b, 10a.
- *Q3*: For comments, ask them to choose just one.
- *Q5*: Take time with E, you could skip the other parts of this question.
- *Q6*: Our desires are deceitful—these lies corrupt our souls.
- *Day 5*: Important—be sure to get to these!

LESSON 3: WHY ONLY SOME WILL BE SET FREE

- Information-gathering questions that could be skipped in discussion: 1b, 5, 8.
- *Q3c*: Believing God loved her is key to helping her wait on Him to meet her.
- *Q7b*: For example, people who gossip, make racist comments, are gluttonous in food or drink, spend money frivolously . . .
- *Q9b*: Hear from many on this one—you can't practice soul talk too often!

LESSON 4: A SHOCKING METAPHOR

When I've done this study with others, I've found that women had much to say in response to these questions, and many had never studied these passages. For that reason I don't think you should skip questions. I would also suggest doing this lesson over two weeks, with the first twelve questions for the first week. Then you will have no video the second week and you can finish the questions.

- **Q3a**: Our idols promise to do for us what we think God will not. In Gomer's case, her lovers provided for her and then sold her, naked, on the auction block. This vivid picture must not be missed.
- **Q3e, 5c,** and **8**: Be sure to take enough time with these.
- **Q13b**: "Arise, my love"—God wants a bride who wants to be with Him. He also wants, according to verse 14, to hear our voice and see our face.

LESSON 5: OUR CHEATING HEARTS

- Information-gathering questions that could be skipped in discussion: 2b, 6, 13.
- **Q8b**: All of this is intervention language—trying to make the women face the truth that the cost for listening to idols is high.
- **Q8c**: A swift she-camel leaves tracks all over the desert when she is in heat, running until her feet are sore and she is spent with thirst. And yet—she cannot rest.
- **Q10c**: Another good chance to practice soul talk.
- **Q12**: Jeremiah 3:25 is the language of true repentance, when you admit not only that you were wrong, but you are willing to see the pain it has brought both to you and your God.
- **Q14a**: A pure virgin—particularly not following after false teachers.

- **Q14b**: Willing to put God over being with the people you love most.

LESSON 6: WHEN THE EARTH SHAKES

- Information-gathering questions that could be skipped in discussion: 4, 8.
- **Q3**: The story of Ananias and Sapphira, though shocking, should awaken us to the futility of our idols. It also demonstrates that we are part of a body, and if we are trusting in idols, God may need to shake our world to purify the body. Questions in your group may arise about their eternal salvation. Only God knows the state of their souls. We do not know if they were eternally lost because they never really knew Him or if they lost only their earthly lives.
- **Q9a**: Her assertiveness (in contrast to Mary falling at His feet) seems to indicate rebuke, some control issues still alive.
- **Q9b** and **9c**: Martha thinks of resurrection as "coming in the future," but Jesus makes it clear than when we believe, resurrection life begins immediately spiritually.
- **Q10b**: In the Hebrew, the verbs indicate wrath on the part of Christ. He seemed to be thinking of more than just this death, which He would quickly turn around. Perhaps He was grieving for all the funerals He would not stop.
- **Q12b**: We know God's wrath fell on Christ for our sins and that God had to look away. Perhaps this was the Father's grief and anger at the price that had to be paid.
- **Q13** and **14**: Be sure you get to these questions.

LESSON 7: WHY WE CAN'T JUST SAY NO

- This lesson is intensely practical and involves practicing a lot of soul talk. Hear the soul talk, especially from questions 3b, 4c, and 11c.
- Information-gathering questions that could be skipped in discussion: 2, 4a, 4b, 5, 7a, 7b, 9, 13, 16.
- **2**: Avoid a discussion on water baptism itself but focus on how it pictures death and resurrection.

LESSON 8: IDOLS CANNOT BE REMOVED, ONLY REPLACED

- The following questions are information-gathering questions and have many parts: 5, 6, and 8. Don't take too long with these, but take a few comments.
- *Day Two*: Stop only briefly here, if at all, and then move to the heart of the story of Rachel and Leah.
- *Day Three*: If your meeting place has Internet access, you could show Bonnie Rait singing "I Can't Make You Love Me" on You-Tube. It will set the scene for what you want to emphasize: the pain our idols cause. Go to the heart of idolatry, to the goodness of God, and to ways He blessed Leah (question 9).
- *Day Four*: This is an important day. Slow down.
- *Day Five*: Emphasize 15c, 16, and 17.

LESSON 9: RESPONDING TO OUR ONE TRUE LOVER

- **Q1**: Have someone summarize what is happening, but have many respond to 1c. Some have seen this passage positively, thinking of the bride hiding in the clefts as hiding in Christ. But that doesn't work, since the Bridegroom represents Christ and is asking her to come out, to come higher.

- **Q2**: As Tim Keller says, "A sense of His absence is a sense of His presence."
- *Day 2*: Since question 6 is a review, just answer 6b. Also, just answer 7c.

LESSON 10: WHAT ANGELS LONG TO SEE

- **Q3**: The gospel should assure the "lowly" brother of God's love and should also humble the "rich" brother.
- *Day 3*: You could have someone summarize answers to 9 and 10, but get several responses for 9d and 10f.
- *Days 4 and 5*: Pace yourself to get here—these are important days. Have everyone answer 16 and close with a time of praise.

ACKNOWLEDGMENTS

To my sisters who tested this study (on the blog and face-to-face):
You confessed your heart idols, opened your hearts for
radical surgery, and then encouraged us all with stories
of transformation. Though you are "behind the scenes" I
want others to know I couldn't have done this without
you. It's been thrilling to see firsthand what the Stonecutter is doing.

To Elisa Stanford:
Once I found you, I didn't want any other editor
because you make my writing better. Even before you
experienced your own severe mercy you were wonderful, but now—oh! Your heart is as big as your talent.
May He give us more journeys together!

To my agent, Kathy Helmers:
So thankful for your thoughtful input and for leading me
to Worthy publishers!

To Kris Bearss and the team at Worthy:
I respect each member of this team of immense quality,
but I am deeply thankful to Kris. Kris, you are wise, you
care, and you are impacting lives.

To David, my son-in-law:

Thank you for overcoming my resistance to blogging, and for all the ways you are helping me keep up with this techy generation.

To Tim Keller:

You were the first to open my eyes to heart idols. When I told you I had listened to a sermon a day for seven years, you said, "Do I have that many?" You do—but I pray for many, many more.

NOTES

1. It is a misnomer to call David's sin with Bathsheba adultery, for it was one-sided and he used his power as king to "call for her."

2. Jim Om, "Models of Manipulation" (sermon, Redeemer Presbyterian Church, New York, January 3, 1999). This sermon is available at http://sermons.redeemer.com/store/index.cfm/product/17298/models-of-manipulation.cfm.

3. Walter Wangerin Jr., *The Book of God: The Bible as a Novel* (Grand Rapids, MI: Zondervan, 1996), 741.

4. Charles Swindoll, "Getting Through the Tough Stuff of Anxiety," *Insight for Living*, December 27–28, 2010.

5. Paul Tripp, *Whiter Than Snow* (Wheaton, IL: Crossway, 2008), 104, 84. Used by permission.

6. George Barna, *The Barna Report 1992–1993: America Renews Its Search for God, An Annual Survey of Lifestyles, Values, and Religious Views* (Delight, AR: Gospel Light Publications, 1993), 113.

7. In Homer's *Odyssey*, Scylla looks from a distance like a dangerous rock shoal but is in actuality a six-headed sea monster. Her long necks stretch down to the ship, seizing six of Odysseus's sailors.

8. Tim Keller of Redeemer Presbyterian Church in New York City has identified these categories and gives credit to the teaching he received at the Christian Counseling and Educational Foundation at Westminster Theological Seminary.

9. Dr. Martyn Lloyd-Jones, *Spiritual Depression: Its Causes and Cure* (Grand Rapids, MI: Eerdmans, 1965), 12, 54–56.

10. Augustus M. Toplady, "Rock of Ages," 1898. Alternative lyric: "Save me from wrath and make me pure."

11. Edward Mote, "The Solid Rock," 1834.

12. David Powlison, "How to Keep Ourselves from Idolatry," Christian Counseling & Educational Foundation, January 10, 2012, http://www.ccef.org/video/keeping-ourselves-idol-worship.

13. C. S. Lewis, *The Voyage of the* Dawn Treader (New York: Macmillan, 1952), 90.

14. David Clarkson, *Soul Idolatry: Excludes Men Out of Heaven* (1864; repr., Minneapolis: Curiosmith, 2010), 12.

15. Ibid., 13.

16. The Christian Counseling and Educational Foundation is an organization seeking to restore Christ to counseling and counseling to the Church.

17. A. W. Tozer, *That Incredible Christian* (Camp Hill, PA: Christian Publications, 1986), chap. 34.

18. Jonathan Aitken, *John Newton: From Disgrace to Amazing Grace* (Wheaton, IL: Crossway, 2007), 99.

19. This is quoted many places, and I don't know where the original source was, but it is often credited to Jack Miller, who was with New Life Presbyterian churches, Westminster Theological Seminary, and World Harvest Mission.

20. Philip Yancey, *The Bible Jesus Read* (Grand Rapids, MI: Zondervan, 1999), 179.

21. John Koessler, "Disappointed with Intimacy," *Christianity Today*, November 2011, 34.

22. Dee Brestin, "Viewpoints," *Christianity Today*, January 2012, 53.

23. Quoted in "Blaise Pascal: Scientific and Spiritual Prodigy," *Christianity Today*, August 8, 2008, http://www.christianitytoday.com/ch/131christians/evangelistsandapologists/pascal.html.

24. Carolyn Weber, *Surprised by Oxford* (Nashville: Thomas Nelson, 2011), 2–3.

25. C. S. Lewis, *Mere Christianity* (New York: HarperCollins, 1952), 96.

26. Michael Card, interview by Dee Brestin, "The God of All Comfort, Part 9," *Midday Connection*, August 22, 2011, http://www.moodyradio.org/brd_ProgramDetail.aspx?id=74330.

27. A. W. Tozer, *The Pursuit of God*, Kindle eBook, chap. 1.

28. Ann Voskamp, *One Thousand Gifts* (Grand Rapids, MI: Zondervan, 2010), 217-18.

29. Tim Keller, "Sex and the End of Loneliness" (sermon, Redeemer Presbyterian Church, New York, February 25, 1996).

30. Derek Kidner, *The Message of Jeremiah* (Downers Grove, IL: InterVarsity Press, 1987), 30.

31. Kevin Cawley, February 6, 2011, sermon, Redeemer Fellowship, Kansas City, MO, *Pentateuch 4 Numbers*.

32. Bernard of Clairvaux, *On the Song of Songs*, vol. IV, sermon 76, quoted in Ralph Martin, *The Fulfillment of All Desire* (Steubenville, OH: Emmaus Road Publishing, 2006), 117. Bernard of Clairvaux was a French abbot (1090–1153) and the primary founder of the reforming Cistercian order. John Calvin and other Reformers often quoted him.

33. Derek Kidner, *The Message of Jeremiah* (Downers Grove, IL: InterVarsity Press, 1987), 33 N.4.

34. Nicholas D. Kristof and Sheryl WuDunn, *Half the Sky* (New York: Vintage, 2010), 38.

35. Timothy Keller, *The Reason for God* DVD Curriculum, session 4: "Why Does God Allow Suffering?" (Grand Rapids, MI: Zondervan, 2010).

36. Sheldon Vanauken, *A Severe Mercy, Davy's Edition* (New York: Harper & Row, 1977), 27.

37. Ibid., 35.

38. Ibid., 136.

39. Ibid., 210.

40. Joni Eareckson Tada and Steven Estes, *When God Weeps* (Grand Rapids, MI: Zondervan, 1997), 56.

41. Edmund P. Clowney and Timothy J. Keller, "Preaching Christ in a Postmodern World," 2010. This recording is available at http://itunes.apple.com /itunes-u/preaching-christ-in-postmodern/id378879885#ls=1.

42. R. C. Sproul, "Before Abraham Was, I AM," cassette 6 of *Knowing Christ* (Orlando, FL: Ligonier Ministries, 1999).

43. St. Augustine, *Confessions*, trans. Henry Chadwick (Oxford, UK: Oxford University Press, 1992), 140.

44. It's called *The Rescue* and it is available at deebrestin.com to download or in print and video form for a donation to discipleshipunlimited.org.

45. Walter Wangerin, *The Book of God* (Grand Rapids, MI: Zondervan, 1996), 46.

46. In *The God of All Comfort*, I tell the various ways in which God awakened me to the truth that Steve could not be my rock—and how it was a severe mercy, for God knew He was going to take Steve home early.

47. James Noriega, as quoted in Mike Wilderson, *Redemption* (Wheaton, IL: Crossway, 2011), 38.

48. I post a list of book and movie recommendations on my website, dee brestin.com.

49. A. W. Tozer, *The Pursuit of God*, (Harrisburg, PA: Christian Publications, 1948), Kindle eBook, chap. 7.

50. Leslie Williams, *The Seduction of Lesser Gods* (Nashville: Thomas Nelson, 1997), 12.

51. Hudson Taylor, *Intimacy with Jesus: Understanding the Song of Solomon* (Littleton, CO: OMF International, 2000), 36, 12.

52. Oswald Chambers, "Where the Battle Is Won or Lost," devotion for December 27 in *My Utmost for His Highest* (Crewe, UK: Oswald Chambers Publications, 1992).

53. Madeleine L'Engle, *Penguins and Golden Calves* (Colorado Springs, CO: WaterBrook Press, 1996), 60.

54. John Gottman, *Why Marriages Succeed or Fail* (New York: Simon & Schuster, 1995), np.

55. Victor Hugo, *Les Misérables*, (New York: Thomas Y. Crowell & Co., 1887), Kindle eBook, chap. 12.

56. Henri Nouwen, *The Return of the Prodigal Son* (New York: Doubleday, 1992), 4.

57. I came to understand this parable more fully after reading Timothy Keller's *The Prodigal God*.

DEE BRESTIN is the author of *The Friendships of Women*, which has sold more than one million copies, and *Falling in Love with Jesus* (with Kathy Troccoli), which has sold more than 400,000 copies. She is also a Bible teacher, writer, and speaker with a blog and weekly Bible study that is one of the most active on the Internet. She has published more than twenty Bible studies, is a frequent guest on Moody Radio and Focus on the Family, and speaks annually to thousands of women in America and around the world. Dee resides in Missouri and in her cottage in Wisconsin.

WORTHY
PUBLISHING

IF YOU ENJOYED THIS BOOK, WILL YOU CONSIDER SHARING THE MESSAGE WITH OTHERS?

- Mention the book in a Facebook post, Twitter update, Pinterest pin, blog post, or upload a picture through Instagram.

- Recommend this book to those in your small group, book club, workplace, and classes (for study guides and videos, go to www.IdolLies.net).

- Head over to facebook.com/worthypublishing or facebook.com/deebrestin, "LIKE" the page, and post a comment as to what you enjoyed the most.

- Tweet "I recommend reading #IdolLies by @DeeBrestin // @WorthyPub"

- Pick up a copy for someone you know who would be challenged and encouraged by this message.

- Write a book review online.

You can subscribe to Worthy Publishing's newsletter at **worthypublishing.com**.

WORTHY PUBLISHING
FACEBOOK PAGE

WORTHY PUBLISHING
WEBSITE

CPSIA information can be obtained
at www.ICGtesting.com
Printed in the USA
FFOW04n2031280115
10614FF

9 781617 953675